From Rea...

"I really enjoyed this book. It was very informational and concise. I learned a whole lot about Mormonism! Your book really helped me when I had a conversation with some of my friends at school. It helped me a lot and all I can say is wow. This is a really great book for teens."
— Sabrina, 13, Utah

"I learned a lot about the Mormon doctrine and things my friends talk about at school make more sense to me now."
— Vivian, 15, Utah

"This is a great and easy read. I would recommend it to anyone who wants to know more about Mormonism (teen or non-teen). I liked that it wasn't dumbed down. It was understandable but real. All in all, I loved the book and I'm excited to share it with others!"
— Moriah, 22, California

"I think this is a great resource for teens and adults as well. It will help us greatly in our mission training before we go to Utah."
— Jeff Clabaugh, Youth Pastor, California

"This book was very informative. It taught me so much more about Mormonism that I never knew about! This will definitely help me with my future contacts with Mormons."
— Andrew, 12, Nevada

"This book was very helpful to me. I have a much deeper understanding of what Mormons believe."
— Emily, 18, California

"Although the title announces that this book is for 'teens,' it's a valuable book for anyone wanting an introduction to Mormonism, regardless of their age."
— Amazon.com reader

"This concise book lays out the doctrines and beliefs of the LDS Church in simple and honest terminology. And I appreciate that Eric Johnson really reaches out to the people of Mormon faith in truth, love, and kindness."
— Amazon.com reader

Mormonism 101 For Teens

The Religion of the Latter-day Saints Simplified

By Eric Johnson

3rd Printing: June 2019

Mormonism Research Ministry

Mormonism 101 for Teens: The Religion of the Latter-day Saints Simplified
Copyright © 2019 by Eric Johnson
ISBN 978-0-6926-2532-3
Published by Mormonism Research Ministry, Draper, Utah

All rights reserved. No part of this publication can be reproduced, stored in a retrieval system, or transmitted in any form or by any means—for example, electronic, photocopy, recording—without the prior written permission of the publisher. The only example is brief quotations in printed reviews.

The Bible verses quoted in this publication, unless otherwise noted, are taken from the English Standard Version (ESV) Copyright © 2001 by Crossway Books, a publishing ministry of Good News Publishers. All rights reserved. ESV Text Edition 2007.

The author receives no royalties from the sale of this publication.

To sign up for MRM's free bimonthly newsletter, please go onto www.mrm.org and request the PDF version. By mail, the address is

> Mormonism Research Ministry
> Attn: 101 for Teens
> PO Box 1746
> Draper, UT 84092-1746

To sign up for the Johnsons' free monthly newsletter titled "Johnsons' Great Adventures," please email the author: eric@mrm.org

---

Other published works by Eric Johnson

*Answering Mormons' Questions: Ready Responses for Inquiring Latter-day Saints (*co-authored with Bill McKeever) (Grand Rapids: Kregel, 2013).

Mormonism 101: Examining the Religion of the Latter-day Saints (co-authored with Bill McKeever) (Grand Rapids: Baker Book House, 2015).

Sharing the Good News with Mormons (co-edited with Sean McDowell) (Eugene, OR: Harvest House Publisher Publishers, 2018).

Contributor to the *Apologetics Study Bible for Students* (including the Twisted Scripture entries and several feature articles found throughout this Bible) (Nashville: Holman Publishers, 2009).

Dedication and Appreciation

"Rejoice in the Lord always; again I will say, rejoice."
Philippians 4:4 [1]

Teaching has been my passion for more than a quarter century. With that in mind, *Mormonism 101 for Teens* is dedicated to the several thousand students who have been in my classrooms beginning in 1989 when Terri (my wife and ministry partner since 1988) and I taught a fifth grade Sunday School class at Clairemont Emmanuel Baptist Church (San Diego).

To many of my students at Christian High School of El Cajon, CA whom I taught from 1998-2010 in Bible classes ... thank you for proving that it's possible for teenagers to own their *own* faith. Please know that much of my philosophy in Christian education comes from the many hours I spent with you. I also owe much to former colleague Craig Breuninger, a treasured friend whose regular interaction with me during these years (specifically 1993-2005 when he taught at CHS) intellectually stimulated my thinking, even those rare times when we disagreed. Our many discussions, brainstorming sessions, and "fire chats" deeply influenced my teaching philosophy.

I cannot forget my daughters—Carissa, Janelle, and Hannah—whom I have taught informally over the years. Each has taken the fundamentals of this starter course to the real world, having a number of interactions with Latter-day Saints, including many of their friends. They realize what it means to speak the truth in love, even when there is disagreement on crucial issues. I am very impressed with each one of you. A special thank you to Carissa as well as MRM's Sharon Lindbloom and Bill McKeever for their editing suggestions on this project. Your help is greatly appreciated! I also want to thank Pastor Ritch Sandford from the Mission Church (South Jordan, UT) who graciously designed the book's cover as well as the illustration on page 14. Your skills are top notch!

Finally, I would like to acknowledge my family's prayer and financial supporters. We could not be in Utah without you!

---

[1] Although the official version of the Bible used by Mormons is the King James Version (KJV), I have decided to quote from the English Standard Version (unless otherwise noted), which is more understandable to the average reader. I encourage skeptical Latter-day Saint readers to look up the verses in the KJV to see that the meaning will essentially be the same.

Something to think about before you read

I'm curious. Why did you decide to open the pages to this book? Do you want to gather information to better understand the Mormon religion? Or maybe a parent wants you to read it. (Hopefully you're not being forced to do this against your will!) Could it be you just want to learn how to win arguments with your Mormon friends or neighbors?

My hope is that you would read this book because you know people who are Mormon or you have had missionaries knock on your door. In prior encounters, you may have become confused and didn't really understand what Mormonism teaches. By learning what Mormons believe and how they think, a resource like this can prepare you for these future conversations.

However, if you're just wanting tips on how to destroy your Mormon "opponent" in debate situations, you've picked the wrong resource. (In fact, if this is the main reason why you've decided to read, I might suggest just putting this book down because I have not written it for such a purpose.) Some Christians may think that, by shutting down their "opponents," they win. Actually, this attitude will only cause you (and your message) to lose. It is a different mindset than what is commanded in the Bible. My life verses are 1 Peter 3:15-16:

> But in your hearts set apart Christ as Lord. Always be prepared to give an answer to everyone who asks you to give the reason for the hope that you have. But do this with gentleness and respect, keeping a clear conscience, so that those who speak maliciously against your good behavior in Christ may be ashamed of their slander. (NIV)

Ephesians 4:15 says to "speak the truth" before adding these important words: *"in love."* Understanding what Mormonism is all about is crucial. But communicating truth with gentleness, respect, and love are not optional ingredients according to the apostles Peter and Paul.

If your goal is to better share your Christian faith with Mormons, then I think this might be a valuable resource for you. May the Lord richly bless you as you study this book!

Table of Contents

Introduction — 1

Section I: The Worldview of Mormonism — 7

Chapter 1: Examining the Language of Mormonism — 9
Chapter 2: Examining the Founder of Mormonism — 19
Chapter 3: Examining the Attraction of Mormonism — 29

Section II: The Doctrines of Mormonism — 37

Chapter 4: Examining the God of Mormonism — 39
Chapter 5: Examining the Scriptures of Mormonism — 48
Chapter 6: Examining the Salvation of Mormonism — 56

Section III: The Relationships in Mormonism — 69

Chapter 7: Examining the Educational System of Mormonism — 71
Chapter 8: Examining the Dating System of Mormonism — 83
Chapter 9: Examining the Ways of Sharing Your Faith
 With Mormons — 87

Conclusion: A Final Word to Christian Teens and their Parents — 92

Appendices

1: Recognizing Poor Logic — 94
2: What Must a Person Do in Order to Have a Relationship
 with God? — 98
3: 10 Things An Investigator Ought to Consider Before
 Becoming a Mormon — 100
4: 7 Questions Your Mormon Friend May Ask (with responses) — 102
5: Why Do So Many Mormons Turn to Atheism? — 104

Index — 106

Introduction
Fast Facts on Mormonism

Church Name	The Church of Jesus Christ of Latter-day Saints (LDS, Mormon), the religion's official title since 1838 (D&C 115:3-4). The followers are nicknamed "Mormons," a word that will be used throughout this book along with "LDS" when referring to the organization or its members.
Date Founded	April 6, 1830
LDS Church Founder	Joseph Smith, Jr. (1805-1844)
Headquarters	Salt Lake City, UT (Temple Square, the Conference Center, and the Church Administration Building are located here).
Mormon Population	As of 2019, there are more than 16 million followers, growing by about a million members every four years. More than half of all Mormons live outside the U.S.
Mormonism's Top Leaders	The top leaders of the Mormon Church are the First Presidency, which is made up of the president (prophet) along with his two counselors; the twelve apostles; and the seventy. These leaders are called general authorities or, simply, the "Brethren." Faithful Mormons are supposed to obey their teachings.
General Conference	Held biannually (the first weekends of April and October). Each general conference is made up of five different sessions at the Conference Center in Salt Lake City (across the street from Temple Square) where the leaders and others speak authoritatively on a variety of issues. Many LDS families watch the sessions in person or on TV.
Mormon Missionaries	As of 2018, about 65,000 missionaries, mainly older teenagers, are sent out by the church each year. The males, called elders, are eligible to go on 2-year missions at the age of 18 while the females, called sisters, serve 18 months beginning at the age of 19. Although it's not a requirement to go on a mission, many young people feel peer pressure to do so.
Seminary	Local Mormon teenagers may attend "seminary" classes at a church building near the high school and learn about the church's scriptural doctrines and history. Outside Utah and Idaho, seminary is typically held before or after school. Utah and some Idaho public schools, meanwhile, hold "release time" classes throughout the school day.

Dad, I don't get it. Why do you care so much about the Mormons and their religion?"

It was a legitimate question asked by my oldest daughter Carissa who was about 14 years old at the time. Beginning in 2005, my wife Terri and I were thinking about moving our family from Southern California to the state of Utah to become full-time Christian missionaries in the state of Utah. Since 1989, I had volunteered for Bill McKeever, the founder of Mormonism Research Ministry (a Christian outreach). Bill and his wife Tammy later left Southern California for Utah in 2004. Thinking about leaving "home" for a different state was difficult, since moving would mean our children would have to leave their Christian school. This idea didn't make sense to Carissa. Actually, the idea probably sounded crazy to a number of our friends and family.

Carissa (12) and Hannah (6) hold website signs in 2005 outside the Newport Beach (CA) temple open house.

Terri and I have never been members of The Church of Jesus Christ of Latter-day Saints (nicknamed Mormons, or LDS for short). And we personally knew few Mormons, although a number of Terri's relatives *are* members of this religion. Terri and I first met on a Christian missions trip during the summer of 1987 in Salt Lake City, Utah, out of all places. Within a few months of dating, I remember telling Terri, "If you marry me, understand that we may live in Utah one day." On April 2, 1988, she agreed to my proposal on the San Diego Zoo Skyfari and we were married just a few months later—August 20, to be exact. For more than a quarter century, Terri has been the perfect companion to me in this ministry, a supportive encourager in every way.

So how did I answer the question posed by my daughter? I reminded her about the time in the Old Testament when God asked Isaiah, "Whom shall I send, and who will go for us?" (6:8). Isaiah replied, "Here I am! Send me." "Honey," I told her, "God has laid it upon my heart to share truth with *sincere* people who are *sincerely* lost, at least in a spiritual sense. There are millions of people belonging to this religion who do their best to obey what they think God wants, but they don't know about His grace and what it means to have their sins forgiven." Needless to say, she didn't appear to be completely convinced.

At the age of 16, Carissa graduated a year early from Christian High School in El Cajon, CA, making it possible for our family to move to Utah in the summer of 2010. She stayed in San Diego for the next year and finished her sophomore year of college before moving into our Sandy, Utah home (less than half an hour away from Salt Lake City) in mid-2011. Carissa found a full-time job at a nearby gym and spent a year with us; her regular interaction with an LDS clientele helped her gain a compassionate love for the Mormon people. For several summers she was willing to get in front of my video camera to help me film some YouTube videos so others could be educated on Mormonism; these videos have been viewed thousands of times over the past few years.

"I think I finally get it," Carissa, 19, told me in 2012. Indeed, I know she "gets it." She sincerely loves the Mormon people! In fact, Carissa was instrumental in bringing a missions team from her large Evangelical Christian university to do evangelism in the state of Utah during her final college semester. (She graduated in May 2016 from Liberty University with a master's degree in English.)

For close to two decades, I had taught high school Bible classes at Christian High, a private school of about six hundred students in grades 7-12. For the majority of these years, the class that I taught was titled "Christian Apologetics," which is nothing more than a fancy way of saying why someone ought to believe in the claims made by Christianity. In the final two months of this course, we covered seven different world religions, including Mormonism. Besides teaching the history and doctrines of the religions, I provided an opportunity for my students to accompany me on weekend trips to mosques, temples, and synagogues. In fact, the Islamic imams, Hare Krishna devotees, and Jewish rabbis were some of my best instructors each year!

One of the most popular trips we took was to the Mormon Battalion Center in the "Old Town" part of San Diego. Each March I called the center to reserve LDS missionaries who would give my intrigued students a tour of their facility and share their faith for several hours. It provided a chance for my group to experience the heartfelt testimonies given by these young men and women—they usually ranged in age from 19 to 21[1]—and consider their sincere claim to truth.

These trips were helpful because my students were able to interact with actual adherents of this faith and observe their sincerity. Those I brought couldn't just roll their eyes and say "this religion is stupid," which was a common reaction many had when making conclusions about the different religions we studied. Instead, these teens had to contemplate what was taught and determine if Mormon doctrine made biblical sense. With the background knowledge I had provided through class lectures and videos, they were given a head start.

Perhaps more than any other religion, Mormonism intrigued these students. Time and time again I was asked, "Mr. Johnson, my Mormon

---

[1] In October 2012, the LDS Church lowered the missionary age to 18 for the males and 19 for the females. Many missionaries now go straight from high school to mission field.

(friends / family members / neighbors) are nice people. How are they different from us?" Perhaps their interest came because they knew Mormons and had positive relationships with them. A number of times I had students pull me aside and ask if I thought they could date Mormons.[2]

That's why I'm so glad you haven chosen this book. By utilizing some quotes from LDS sources—including official teachings from the leadership as found in church manuals and magazines—I hope to clarify the religion to someone who has little to no prior understanding. At the same time, I won't "dumb" down my presentation by writing beneath what the average teenager should be able to understand. After all, my experience shows that teenagers are smarter than many adults give them credit.

There will be tables of terms along with their LDS definitions at the beginning of several chapters. I just want you to remember that these are definitions given by Mormons, so don't think that I agree with them or the theology of Mormonism. I will boldface the words when they are first used in that particular chapter. An index of terms is given in the back of the book to help you find topics quicker.

At the end of each chapter is a paragraph titled "Questions to Ask Your Mormon Friend" to help Christians begin conversations with those Mormons they know. I have also included "5 Points Overview" sections at the end of most chapters as a quick review. Please know that this book can be read out of order. Make this resource your own and let it work for you.

By keeping my ideas simple to fit a book of this size, I may not provide as many details as some readers might like. For those wanting more information, consider the other books that I have coauthored on Mormonism.[3] In addition, I strongly encourage you to visit the MRM website (**www.mrm.org**), a resource where you can learn more by reading the many dozens of articles and viewing the available videos.

A final note. Your Mormon friends might tell you that this book is "anti-Mormon." This term is used in a negative way to refer to someone who disagrees with Mormonism. In effect, they judge the author (that's me) as being someone who hates Mormons, even though they don't know me or may have never read anything I've written.

Their charge is faulty. In the preface to *Mormonism 101*, Bill McKeever and I talked about how disagreement does not equal hatred. Because I feel strongly about this, allow me to recite what Bill and I wrote, changing the first person plural pronouns to first person singular:

---

[2] We'll talk more about this topic in chapter 8.
[3] *Answering Mormons' Questions* (Grand Rapids: Kregel, 2013) and *Mormonism 101* (Grand Rapids: Baker, 2015). Both were written with Bill McKeever. I have used some material from these books in several places throughout this book.

All in all, (I) will do (my) best to be respectful with (my) approach. Know that (I) don't hold any animosity toward Latter-day Saints, many of whom (I) call family, friends, and neighbors. Be assured that (I am) moved with the same compassion felt by the LDS missionaries and lay members who attempt to defend what they believe to be true. While the facts as presented in this book may be ignored by certain readers who would question (my) motives, (I) echo the apostle Paul when he addressed the church of Galatia: "Am I therefore become your enemy, because I tell you the truth?" (Gal. 4:16). This book is the result of (my) concern for those who belong to the LDS faith as well as for those Christians who want to better engage Latter-day Saints in healthy dialogue.[4]

Disagreement should never be taken automatically that the other person's intentions are hateful or mean-spirited. Ideas are only as good as the evidence used to back them up. It is possible to disagree on important issues, including faith, in a loving and kind way. I will emphasize this throughout the rest of these pages.

I am confident that the more you comprehend the differences between Mormonism and Christianity, the more likely you will be able to have intelligent conversations with those Latter-day Saints who attend your school, live in your neighborhood, and even belong to your extended family. May God richly bless you in your endeavors!

5 Points Overview of the Introduction

1. Christians should know what they believe. The message of the Bible—such as God's nature and the importance of faith—should be studied and understood by dedicated believers.
2. Christians need to comprehend others' beliefs. This includes atheism, Islam, and Mormonism. Understanding the background and unique doctrines will help make your conversations worthwhile.
3. Christians ought to be willing to engage others when the opportunity arises. Can you imagine a person who won the lottery not telling anyone? Impossible! Isn't Jesus better than winning millions?
4. Christians will want to have important conversations about faith...but understanding the mindset of others and how terms are defined are essential ingredients in making this possible.
5. Christians must remember that points 1-4 should be accomplished with "gentleness and respect" and loving those who may disagree.

---

[4] *Mormonism 101*, p. 15.

Section I: The Worldview of Mormonism

Above: A view of downtown Salt Lake City and Temple Square in Utah. The Salt Lake Temple (with spires) is toward the front right of the photo. Below: the Salt Lake Temple (foreground) and the Tabernacle behind it to the left.

world·vie̲w
wərldˈvyoo/
noun

a particular philosophy of life or conception of the world.

Chapter 1: Examining the Language of Mormonism

Aaronic Priesthood	A priesthood authority lost soon after biblical times that was restored to the earth through Joseph Smith by John the Baptist in 1829. Today this is given to worthy males who beginning at the age of 11. They can then hold the offices of deacon, teacher, and priest.
Baptism	Immersion of the convert in water, a requirement for the "remission of sins." This ordinance must be officiated by a Mormon male who has priesthood authority.
Celestial Kingdom	The hope of faithful Latter-day Saints is to qualify for eternal life and spend eternity as a family in this place, the highest of three kingdoms of glory.
Celestial Marriage	A marriage taking place in a Mormon temple that lasts for "time" (this life) as well as for "eternity." In the 19th century, these words referred to polygamy (one man, multiple wives), which was a Mormon requirement in earlier days.
Confirmation	A ceremony that takes place after water baptism, making the convert a member of the Mormon Church. Males with priesthood authority lay their hands on the participant who is then told to receive the Holy Spirit.
Council in Heaven	The place in premortality where God the Father's plan for the world was announced, with Jesus chosen to be the Savior of the world.
Deacon	Lowest of four offices in the Aaronic Priesthood given to males beginning at the age of 11 (a change made in 2019).
Enduring to the End	Remaining faithful until death (through keeping commandments) in order to obtain eternal life.
Eternal Progression	Three stages of existence experienced by every human being: first estate (premortality); second estate (mortality); and third estate (immortality).
General Authority	One of the top male leaders in the Mormon Church (prophet/president, apostles, and seventies).
Golden Contact	A non-member of the LDS Church who meets regularly with the Mormon missionaries and is considered a likely convert.

God the Father (Heavenly Father, Elohim)	Once a righteous human being in another realm who died and then became the God of this world. He is a male who has a body of flesh and bones (D&C 130:22).
Great Apostasy	The idea that the universal Christian church lost its authority soon after the death of the apostles and was in need of a complete restoration.
Immortality	A gift given through Jesus to all humans, regardless of their behavior on earth. It provides a person the chance to live forever as resurrected being in one of three kingdoms of glory.
Investigator	A nonmember who is willing to take the missionary lessons in order to consider joining the LDS Church.
Melchizedek Priesthood	A priesthood authority that was lost after biblical times and returned to the earth through Joseph Smith by the apostles Peter, James, and John in 1829. Today this is given to worthy males who hold the office of "elder" beginning at the age of 18.
Mortality	Physical life on this earth that begins at birth and ends at death. Every person should desire eternal life in the next life, which can be found in Mormonism.
Outer Darkness	Severe punishment for eternity, reserved mainly for Satan and the Sons of Perdition—specifically, those spirits who fell in premortality.
Paradise	Temporary state in the post-mortal spirit world for those who remain faithful to Mormonism for the rest of their lives.
Plan of Salvation	Mormonism's explanation for how all spirits were first created in premortality. From there, obedient spirits were given bodies and sent to this earth, known as mortality; the future state will be in one of three kingdoms in post-mortality.
Premortality (Preexistence)	The time before earthly mortality when all humans existed as spirit children, born of relationships between God the Father and Heavenly Mother(s). Jude 1:6 is cited to name this the "first estate."
Postmortality	A temporary state consists of spirit prison and paradise. The final state results in one of three kingdoms of glory: the celestial, terrestrial, or telestial kingdoms. Outer darkness is reserved for Satan and the Sons of Perdition.
Sacrament	Similar to Christianity's communion or the Lord's Supper, this ordinance is performed weekly in LDS services, with bread and water serving as elements.

Sons of Perdition	Two groups: 1) One third of all spirits from premortality who were cast out of heaven because of their disobedience; final destination is Outer Darkness; 2) Humans in this life who turn against God and willfully serve Satan.
Spirit Prison	Temporary place in the post-mortal spirit world reserved for those not faithful in mortality. Living Mormons on earth perform works in LDS temples so these spirits will be allowed to have presentation of the Mormon gospel.
Telestial Kingdom	The lowest kingdom of glory, reserved for the wicked of the world.
Terrestrial Kingdom	The middle kingdom of glory, a place for honorable people who were blinded by Satan's activities.
War in Heaven	Conflict in the premortal life initiated by Lucifer when his plan to become the savior of the world was rejected by God.

Have you ever had trouble communicating with someone who understood particular terms differently than you? For instance, perhaps you became confused when a person from Europe referred to a "football match" and actually meant soccer. Or when you realize that a relative from the Midwest who asks for "pop" isn't looking for your father but rather wants a carbonated cold drink. (In the same way, your Southern relatives requesting a "Coke" may really want Mountain Dew or Diet Pepsi, while those in the Northeast may use the word "soda.") It won't take long to realize that the words your Mormon friend uses may mean something different than what you thought.

A church manual used by LDS missionaries states:

> We have a powerful message with a unique vocabulary. Just as a physician speaks differently in the family waiting room than in the operating room, so too must you learn to speak so that those who are unfamiliar with our message can understand what you are teaching.[1]

These differences need to be understood if meaningful conversations are to take place. For example, consider the word "Christian." At a general conference in 2007, an LDS **general authority** named Gary J. Coleman related the story of 14-year-old Cortnee, the daughter of a local LDS leader, who had asked her mother if Mormons were Christian:

---

[1] *Preach My Gospel: A Guide to Missionary Service* (Salt Lake City: Intellectual Reserve, 2004), p. 21.

As a member of The Church of Jesus Christ of Latter-day Saints, you are a Christian, and I am too. I am a devout Christian who is exceedingly fortunate to have greater knowledge of the true "doctrine of Christ" since my conversion to the restored Church. These truths define this Church as having the fullness of the gospel of Jesus Christ, I now understand the true nature of the Godhead, I have access to additional scripture and revelation, and I can partake of the blessings of priesthood authority. Yes, Cortnee, we are Christians.[2]

Just what did Coleman mean when he used the phrase "restored Church" and "priesthood authority"? To comprehend LDS teaching, it must be understood that Mormonism was founded upon the idea that biblical Christianity lost all divine authority soon after the death of the New Testament apostles. This is called the **Great Apostasy**. Mormon leaders claim that this authority did not return to the earth until April 6, 1830 when Joseph Smith founded the Mormon Church.

Because it is taught that the doctrines of Christians had become corrupted, LDS leaders claim that there was a need for a "restoration." This is why Mormons do not use the statements of faith (creeds) that you may hear recited in many Christian church services, including the Apostles' Creed and the Nicene Creed. When Joseph Smith asked **God the Father** (usually called "Heavenly Father" by the Mormon faithful) for an answer to his prayer regarding which of all the Christian denominations was true, he claimed that he was told how he should not join any of them because "they were all wrong" and how the Christian "creeds were an abomination in his sight" while the Christian pastors were "corrupt."[3]

Thus, when Coleman declared that Mormons "have the fullness of the gospel of Jesus Christ," he meant that divine authority can be found only in Mormonism. While a Mormon may refer to non-Mormons as "Christians," it should be understood that anyone not having the LDS priesthood lacks this authority. One current church manual explains, "Many in the Christian world are sincere, and their false doctrinal conclusions are not their own fault."[4] The LDS priesthood is given only to worthy Mormon males; females are not allowed to receive this authority. Only when a Mormon female is married to a faithful LDS man in a Mormon temple does she receive the benefit of the man's authority.

---

[2] Gary J. Coleman, "Mom, Are We Christians?" *Ensign*, May 2007, p. 94. I will discuss the references to the "Godhead" as well as "additional scripture and revelation" in chapters 4 and 5.
[3] See *Joseph Smith-History* 1:19 found in the LDS scripture Pearl of Great Price.
[4] *Old Testament Student Manual 1 Kings-Malachi Religion 302*, 2003, p. 166.

The first type of authority is called the **Aaronic Priesthood**, which is known as the "lesser priesthood." Mormons believe that Joseph Smith received this through a personal appearance of John the Baptist in 1829. Today worthy males can receive this authority beginning at the age of eleven. Those having this priesthood are called **deacons.** They perform various duties in the LDS Church, including helping serve the weekly **sacrament**, similar to the communion (or the Lord's Supper) celebrated regularly in Christian worship services. Bread and water are the elements used in the LDS ceremony; during the time when these elements are brought to the people's seats by the deacons, faithful Mormons make promises (called covenants) to obey the commandments as defined and taught by the LDS Church leadership.

The higher, or "greater," priesthood is known as the **Melchizedek Priesthood**. Mormons are taught that this authority was given to Joseph Smith sometime in 1829—the exact date is unknown—by the biblical apostles Peter, James, and John. Today Mormon males who are eighteen years and older are able to receive the Melchizedek priesthood, giving them the title "Elder." (Male missionaries who come to your door will wear a name badge with this title listed before their last name; female missionaries have the title "Sister.") Among other duties, those possessing this authority are allowed to lay their hands upon new converts to "bestow the gift of the Holy Ghost" or give blessings to those who need healing, comfort, or counsel.

The Plan of Salvation

In biblical Christianity, heaven is reserved for those whose sins are forgiven, allowing believers to spend eternity with God. Only those who have accepted Jesus as their Lord and Savior are cleansed from all sin—past, present, and future. The relationship that Christians have with God is not based on personal faithfulness or through the accomplishment of good works; rather, salvation is based on faith alone.

This concept is made very clear in Ephesians 2:8-9, which says it is "by grace you have been saved through faith. And this is not your own doing; it is the gift of God, not a result of works, so that no one may boast." Meanwhile, the Bible teaches that those who do not have a personal relationship with God will spend eternity separated from Him forever.

These teachings are understood differently in Mormonism. To understand the **Plan of Salvation**, let's back up for a moment and discuss what **eternal progression** means. Mormons are taught that there are three states of development: the first estate (**premortality**), the second estate (**mortality**), and the third estate (**postmortality**).

The first estate is where all human beings once existed as spirit children of God the Father. According to Mormonism, all human be-

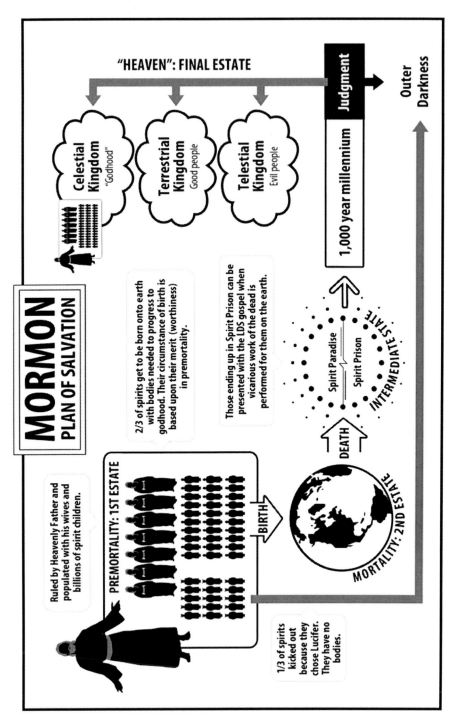

Illustration by Ritch Sandford

ings lived in **premortality** (also called the preexistence) before they were born on Earth. When God's plan for the earth was announced at the **Council in Heaven**, each spirit child had to decide who should be the savior of earth: Lucifer or Jesus. Jesus was the correct choice because he was the firstborn spirit child of God and had the right to this position.

Unfortunately, one-third of the spirits in premortality chose Lucifer (also known as Satan, the spirit brother of Jesus) and his corrupt plan. These spirits—in essence, the spiritual brothers and sisters of all human beings—were cast out of God's presence when Jesus was victorious in the succeeding **War in Heaven**; hence, the followers of Lucifer were prohibited from entering the earth with physical bodies and are now called the **sons of perdition**.

The other two-thirds of the spirits—you and me included—chose Jesus and were given the ability to be born on Earth (**mortality**, or the second estate) with physical bodies. Because of Adam's "transgression" of God's commandment (2 Nephi 2:25 in the Book of Mormon says that "Adam fell that men might be"), these obedient spirits were permitted to come to earth to experience "mortal probation." This allowed all people on earth to have agency, which is the freedom to choose (or reject) the LDS gospel.[5]

Postmortality is the realm where all human spirits go after death. Each person's spirit will immediately go to one of two temporary places in the spirit world: either **spirit prison** or **paradise**. Spirit prison is a place for deceased non-Mormons or unrighteous Mormons who await temple work done on their behalf by living Mormons. It is here where "spirit missionaries" from paradise will share the message of the "restored gospel" to those needing it. Every soul in spirit prison will be given an opportunity to receive this message through the work accomplished by living Mormons in one of the many LDS temples.[6]

After the final judgment, Mormonism teaches that there will be four possible places for a soul to be sent. **Outer darkness** is where Satan and the sons of perdition (humanity's former spiritual brothers and sisters in premortality) will spend eternity; in addition, this is where those Mormons who willfully and deliberately denied the Holy Ghost and Mormonism—even though they knew it was true—will dwell. While this might be considered similar to the Christian "hell," few people (if anyone) will actually go there. Even infamous Nazi leader Adolph Hitler had work done for him in a Mormon temple long after he was dead;[6] thus, for several decades this dictator has been eligible to have the LDS gospel presented to him in spirit prison. If he can possibly receive this teaching, who can't?

---

[5] Before 1978, those with black skin were considered "less valiant" and were prohibited from having priesthood authority. Their deeds in premortality were said to be the cause. For more information on this historical topic, go to www.mrm.org/the-priesthood.

[6] See chapter 7 to read more on the temple.

Because of what Jesus accomplished on the earth, **immortality** is provided to humans, allowing them to receive one of three kingdoms, or degrees of glory. The lowest level is called the **telestial kingdom**, a place reserved for the wicked of this world. The middle level is the **terrestrial kingdom**, a comfortable location where honorable people who had been blinded by Satan's activities will spend eternity. Finally, there is the **celestial kingdom**, which is a place reserved for those who participated in a temple marriage ceremony (called **celestial marriage**) while repenting of all sins and doing everything the LDS leaders say must be done, including **enduring to the end**. In essence, eternal life is the ability for a man and his wife to attain "godhood" while possessing "all divine attributes" and "doing as God does and being as God is."[7] Thus, when a Mormon says that "families are forever," this saying is meant in quite a literal fashion.

5 Points Overview of Chapter 1

1. Many religious terms used by Mormons are also used by Christians. However, there are usually big differences in the meanings, which can cause confusion.
2. Defining terms is important. To avoid confusion, ask your Mormon friends to explain what they mean when they use words such as *God*, *scripture*, and *salvation by grace*.
3. According to Mormonism's doctrine of the Great Apostasy, there was a complete falling away of Christianity soon after the death of the biblical apostles. Divine authority was then said to be returned to the earth through Joseph Smith in 1829.
4. Your male Mormon friends who are at least 11 years old probably possess the Aaronic Priesthood; those who are 18 may also have the Melchizedek Priesthood.
5. The Plan of Salvation covers humanity's past, present, and future. The goal is to attain exaltation in the celestial kingdom where it is believed that families can be together forever.

---

[6] Check out the temple work done on behalf of Hitler: www.mrm.org/adolph-hitler-record.
[7] *The Encyclopedia of Mormonism*, 1:273. More on this topic will be covered in chapter 7.

Questions to Ask Your Mormon Friend

The idea that there are important differences between Mormonism and Christianity was pointed out at the April 2016 general conference by Bonnie L. Oscarson, the Young Women's General President. In her talk she said:

> We claim that The Church of Jesus Christ of Latter-day Saints is the kingdom of God and the only true Church on the earth. It is called the Church of Jesus Christ because He stands at the head; it is His Church, and all these things are possible because of His atoning sacrifice. We believe that these distinguishing features can be found in no other place or organization on this earth. As good and sincere as other religions and churches are, none of them have the authority to provide the ordinances of salvation that are available in The Church of Jesus Christ of Latter-day Saints.[8]

There are three main points given by Oscarson:

1) The only "true Church on the earth" is the LDS Church.
2) Jesus stands at this church's head.
3) No other church has God's authority, no matter how nice it is.

Your Mormon friends may ask if you think they are "Christian." If you attempt to answer honestly, they could become angry and may want to argue. Rather than debate this issue, ask, *"Do you agree that there are major differences between our faiths?"* Explain that there are only four possibilities when Mormonism is compared to biblical Christianity:

1. *Both Mormonism and biblical Christianity are true.* Yet if the teachings of the two faiths are contradictory, only *one* view can be true. Show your friend the Oscarson quote above to show how this cannot be a valid option.
2. *Both Mormonism and biblical Christianity are far from the ultimate truth.* This is possible. Other viable truth options might be Buddhism, Islam, or even atheism. Perhaps one of these is more in line with reality than Christianity or Mormonism. Neither Mormons nor Christians think this is true.
3. *Mormonism is more closely aligned with the truth than biblical Christianity.* If correct, Joseph Smith is a true prophet and everyone should convert.
4. *Biblical Christianity is more closely aligned with the truth than Mormonism.* This possibility makes Mormonism false and therefore in error.

Truth is narrow! Thus, only one of the two faiths—Mormonism or Christianity—can be true for all people in all times and in all places. The other view is wrong. A Mormon should be willing to address the differences because so much is at stake. In turn, a Christian ought to be patient and give clear explanations. This is what productive dialoguing is all about!

---

[8] "Do I Believe?" *Ensign*, May 2016, p. 88.

What About the Missionaries?

Your LDS friends may try to set up a meeting between you and the Mormon missionaries. It is up to you (and your parents) whether or not to meet with them. (If so, perhaps your parents would like to sit in on the meeting.)

Missionaries travel in pairs on foot, on bikes, or in cars. The males dress in collared shirts and slacks while wearing badges that say "Elder"; the females are called "Sisters" and will either wear dresses/skirts or nice slacks. The perceived maturity of the missionaries can be intimidating. Understand, however, that most male missionaries are 18-20 years old while the females are normally 19-20. Many just graduated from high school.

The missionaries study a church manual that shows them how to teach **investigators**, or potential converts. Published in 2004, the manual is titled *Preach My Gospel*. Included in this large book are lessons on doctrinal topics, including the "Great Apostasy," the "Restoration of the Gospel of Jesus Christ," "the Plan of Salvation," "the Gospel of Jesus Christ," and "the Commandments." The manual provides a general overview on some of Mormonism's most important doctrines and policies.

The goal of this 228-page resource is to instruct the missionaries on how to help potential converts "make commitments and prepare for **baptism** and **confirmation**." The term **golden contact** has been used by some to describe someone who is likely to convert to Mormonism. Once the convert has been water baptized, the ordinance of confirmation will be scheduled at the chapel. When complete, the person officially becomes a member of the LDS Church.

With that being said, you need to understand that the missionaries' "duty" is to convince others that this church is true. If you decide to meet with the missionaries, explain how determining truth is the most important thing that anyone can do. Be sure to ask for definitions of the terms they use. (Hopefully, *Mormonism 101 for Teens* will help you better comprehend the meanings of the vocabulary we share.)

When in doubt, be sure to ask, "What do you mean by that?" While there is nothing wrong with meeting the missionaries to learn more about Mormonism from the official representatives of the LDS Church, be cautious as the missionaries will do everything they can to baptize you into their church. Be kind and fair, but be aware as well.

Chapter 2: Examining the Founder of Mormonism

LDS Names, Places, and Terms (in order of use in this chapter)

Joseph Smith, Jr.	(1805-1844) Founder of the LDS religion.
First Vision	Officially understood as the appearance of God the Father and Jesus Christ to Joseph Smith in 1820.
Moroni	The son of Mormon and the last living Nephite in the Book of Mormon. He buried gold plates containing the Book of Mormon in upstate New York and later appeared as an angel to Joseph Smith. A golden statue of Moroni blowing a trumpet is located on a spire at most LDS temples.
Nephites	A Book of Mormon people group on the American continent that was generally righteous but annihilated by the Lamanites (the wicked people) in the 5th century A.D.
Lamanites	A Book of Mormon people group on the American continent that was generally wicked and eventually destroyed the Nephites.
Mormon	An ancient Nephite prophet and father of Moroni who compiled the records of the American people into the Book of Mormon. This is also a nickname for a Latter-day Saint.
Book of Mormon	"Another Testament of Jesus Christ" compiled by Moroni on gold plates and later buried. Joseph Smith was given access to the plates, translating them and printing the scripture in 1830. Missionaries encourage potential converts to read the Book of Mormon and pray about its message to see if it (and the religion) is true.
Oliver Cowdery	A good friend to Joseph Smith and one of the Three Witnesses to the Book of Mormon. Served as the primary scribe to Smith, writing down the words dictated to him.
Independence, MO	A city where the Mormons settled temporarily in the late 1830s. Joseph Smith predicted that Jesus would appear in this city at the Second Coming.
Nauvoo, IL	Formerly known as Commerce, a place that was settled by the Mormons in 1839. Most Latter-day Saints left here with Brigham Young in 1846.

Nauvoo Expositor	A 4-page one-time newspaper dated June 7, 1844. It was produced by former Mormons who were not happy with Joseph Smith and described problems they saw in Mormonism, including Smith's polygamy. The paper's printing press was destroyed, for which Smith was arrested.
Polygamy / Plural Marriage	One man married to two (or more) girls/women. This was a practice in Mormonism until 1890 and is no longer an official doctrine.
Carthage Jail	The jail where Joseph Smith and his brother Hyrum were held and then killed in a gun battle on June 26, 1844.

To get a better understanding on the claims made by a particular religion, it is important to learn more about the founder and study the faith's history. For Buddhism, it is important to study the life of Siddhartha Gautama; for Islam, Muhammad should be the focus; and for the Hare Krishna movement, A. C. Bhaktivedanta Swami Prabhupada ought to be considered. With that in mind, let's take a closer look at **Joseph Smith**.

Smith was born on December 23, 1805 to a farming couple in Sharon, Vermont. The family later settled thirty miles east of Rochester, New York, in a town called Palmyra. While they do not worship their founder, Mormons today view Joseph Smith as an authentic prophet in the "latter days" chosen by God to "restore" Christianity.

While there have been nine different **First Vision** accounts, most Mormons are familiar with the version that originated in 1838 and was later published in 1842. It reports how fourteen-year-old Smith wanted to know which of all the Christian churches in his area of New York was true. He claimed that a passage from the New Testament epistle of James led him to a grove of trees near his family's farm in 1820 where two personages (God the Father and Jesus Christ) visited him. According to the account written down in the LDS scripture Pearl of Great Price (chapter 1 of Joseph Smith—History), these personages told Smith that all of the Christian churches were wrong, their creeds (teachings) were an abomination, and their leaders were corrupt. The First Vision is a cornerstone event of the religion of Mormonism.

Smith reported how the local pastors did not believe in his message. Still, Smith insisted that his vision of God the Father and Jesus was true. One night in 1823, Smith—now 17—said he was praying in the bedroom that he shared with his siblings when he received another heavenly visit, this time from an angel who introduced himself as **Moroni**.

During his earthly life, Moroni is described as a great warrior who lived among a righteous ancient people group called **Nephites** (the generally wicked people group were known as **Lamanites**). He was a descendant of a Jewish family that escaped the capture of Jerusalem by sailing across the ocean to the Western Hemisphere about 600 years before the birth of Jesus. It was allegedly this same Moroni who, prior to his death, buried a set of gold plates compiled by his father (**Mormon**) on which was inscribed a record of the ancient American people. Smith was chosen to retrieve that record, but it was several years before he was given permission by the angel to do so. Moroni is said to have appeared to Smith on several other occasions until the time finally came to retrieve the Nephite record.

On September 22, 1827, Joseph Smith—now almost 22 years old—was entrusted with the gold plates. Later he began translating the "Reformed Egyptian" characters into English. The scripture that Mormons believe Smith translated is the **Book of Mormon**. Eventually a total of eleven men were chosen to "see" the gold plates, although some later confessed that they only saw them by faith.[1]

In April 1829, Smith was joined by his third cousin **Oliver Cowdery**. A schoolteacher by profession, Cowdery became Smith's main scribe. The two claimed that they were visited by John the Baptist while praying in the woods near the Susquehanna River (Pennsylvania) in May 1829. It was here that both men were ordained and received the Aaronic Priesthood. At a later point in time, they were given the Melchizedek Priesthood by the biblical apostles Peter, James, and John. The exact date of this event is not known.

On April 6, 1830, Joseph Smith founded the "Church of Christ" (not affiliated with the Church of Christ Protestant denomination) with six members. By the end of the year, the church was fifty times bigger, growing to 300 members. In August 1831, a small group of Latter-day Saints moved into an area twelve miles west of **Independence, Missouri.**

Smith prophesied that it was here where the "New Jerusalem" described in the book of Revelation would be built. On August 3, Smith laid a cornerstone for a temple. Even though he predicted that this location would become a gathering place for the Saints waiting for the Second Coming of Jesus Christ, his prophecy was never fulfilled.

Having many Mormon settlers move into the area, coupled with Smith's predictions that "Zion"

A statue depicting the conferring of the Melchizedek Priesthood at Temple Square in Salt Lake City, Utah.

---

[1] For more on this issue, see http://www.mrm.org/eleven-witnesses

A statue of Joseph Smith at Temple Square.

would be established and the time of the "Gentiles" was coming to an end, led to many hard feelings between the Mormons and the non-LDS Missourians. The all-important gathering of the Saints was short-lived. Within three years the Saints were forced to leave Independence, and the temple never became a reality.

The Saints moved north and settled for a while in an area called Far West, Missouri. Smith again predicted that a temple would be built, but eventually the Saints were forced to leave this place as well. Hostilities between the Mormons and their Missouri counterparts erupted in violence. For example, in October 1838, Mormons attacked a group of Missouri militiamen who had held three LDS men. This led to the slaughter of seventeen Latter-day Saints at Haun's Mill one week later. Joseph Smith was arrested and charged with treason. He spent several months in the dungeon of the Liberty (MO) Jail until he was allowed to escape in April of 1839.

In the meantime, the Saints had moved to a swampy area on the banks of the Mississippi River known as Commerce, Illinois. Enduring sickness and disease, they were successful in turning the once uninhabitable land into a city that attracted followers from all areas. Commerce later became the city of **Nauvoo;** within a short period of time, the city rivaled Chicago in size. Even here, trouble followed the Mormons.

The rapid influx of Latter-day Saints to Nauvoo once again made the church both an economic and political threat in the eyes of the local residents. Joseph Smith was elected mayor while several of his close associates came to hold a number of important political offices. Compounding the problem was the increasing number of people who learned to distrust the Mormon prophet. Many of these men were once close advisors to Smith, including some who were successful businessmen in Nauvoo.

Accusations between Smith and his detractors fueled the tension. On June 7, 1844, some of these men printed a first and only edition newspaper called the *Nauvoo Expositor.* As its name implied, the purpose of the paper was to expose Joseph Smith as a false prophet who had exceeded his authority as mayor and was involved with secretly practicing what they termed "spiritual wifery," or **polygamy**.

The Nauvoo city council quickly reacted by declaring the *Expositor* a nuisance. Under the orders of Smith, the city marshal destroyed the offending publication and the printing press as well. Of course, this only upset Smith's enemies all the more. Negative feelings increased immediately in Nauvoo and its neighboring communities. Amid threats of violence against himself and his followers, Smith placed Nauvoo under martial law on June 18, 1844. In doing so, he mobilized the Nauvoo Legion, an army of several thousand Mormon men who had sworn allegiance to protect Smith at all costs.

When news reached Illinois Governor Thomas Ford, he intervened and suggested that Smith order his army to back down. He then ordered Smith to turn himself in to the authorities in nearby Carthage in the hope of settling the many differences that had escalated over the past several days. On June 25, Smith traveled to Carthage, taking up residence at a local hotel. However, he was once again arrested and jailed in the "debtor's cell" at the **Carthage Jail**. With him were his brother Hyrum, John Taylor, and Willard Richards.

On June 26, the Illinois governor went to Smith's cell for a personal interview. After the meeting, Governor Ford traveled to Nauvoo but left a small group of guards known as the Carthage Greys, many of whom were not sympathetic to the Mormon prophet. In the late afternoon of the next day (June 27), a group attacked the jail, rushing up the stairs to Smith's jail cell. Leaning against the door, the jailed men attempted to defend themselves. Smith, who was armed with a pistol that had been smuggled to him by one of his visitors, opened fire on the attackers. His six-shot pistol discharged only three times, but according to eyewitness John Taylor, all three bullets hit their mark.[2]

Still, there was no way that the small group of men could overpower the mob. A musket ball penetrated the cell's wooden door and hit Hyrum in the face. He fell back, with his last words allegedly being "I am a dead man." John Taylor was shot several times but was able to find cover under the bed. According to the official account, Smith then leapt toward the window of the cell where he was shot several times and fell two stories to the ground below. The mob then shot Smith

---

[2] *History of the Church* 7:100. See also *The Gospel Kingdom*, p. 358. Taylor said two of those shot later died.

again. Only Willard Richards escaped without injury. Today Latter-day Saints call Smith a martyr and even "a lamb led to the slaughter."[3]

Joseph Smith's polygamy

These two guns were smuggled into Joseph Smith's jail cell. The top one is a .32 caliber Ethan Allen pepperbox pistol used by Smith in a gun battle, as he shot three of his attackers. The guns are displayed in the Church History Museum near Temple Square in Salt Lake City. (For more on this fascinating museum, see page 38.)

Polygamy, also known as plural marriage, was openly practiced by Latter-day Saints during the second half of the nineteenth century. The Mormon doctrine began with Joseph Smith. The fact that "careful estimates put the number" of Smith's wives "between 30 and 40"—above and beyond his first wife Emma—is admitted on the LDS Church's official website in footnote 24 of the Gospel Topics essay titled "Plural Marriage in Kirtland and Nauvoo."[4] What is even more amazing is that a third of Smith's wives were teenagers when they married Smith. According to Mormon historian Todd Compton,

> eleven (33 percent) were 14 to 20 years old when they married him. Nine wives (27 percent) were twenty-one to thirty years old. Eight wives (24 percent) were in Smith's own peer group, ages thirty-one to forty. In the group aged forty to fifty, there is a substantial drop off: two wives, or 6 percent, and three (9 percent) in the group fifty-one to sixty. The teenage representation is the largest, though the twenty-year and thirty year-groups are comparable, which contradicts the Mormon folk-wisdom that sees the beginnings of polygamy as an attempt to care for older, unattached women.[5]

Notice how more teenagers were married to Smith than any other age! Marrying girls who easily could be his daughters isn't something

---

[3] For more on this issue, check out an article that I had written for the *Christian Research Journal* titled "The Martyrdom of Joseph Smith" (Vol. 31, No. 3, 2008), which can be found at www.mrm.org/martyrdom.
[4] www.lds.org/topics/plural-marriage-in-kirtland-and-nauvoo.
[5] Compton, *In Sacred Loneliness: The Plural Wives of Joseph Smith* (Salt Lake City: Signature Press, 1997), p. 11.

a man in his 30's should be doing. Smith did not limit his secret marriages to those who were single, as another third of his wives were already married to living husbands:

> A common misconception concerning Joseph Smith's polyandry is that he participated in only one or two such unusual unions. In fact, fully one-third of his plural wives, eleven of them, were married civilly to other men when he married them. . . of Smith's first twelve wives, nine were polyandrous. . . . none of these women divorced their "first husbands" while Smith was alive and all of them continued to live with their civil spouses while married to Smith.[6]

It is difficult to justify Smith's practice of marrying other men's wives. Leviticus 20:10 declares that an adulterous act was punishable by death in ancient Israel: "If a man commits adultery with the wife of his neighbor, both the adulterer and the adulteress shall surely be put to death." Besides teenagers and women who were married to living husbands, Smith married a mother and her daughter (Patty Bartlett (Sessions) and Sylvia Porter Sessions Lyons) as well as pairs of sisters (Huntington, Partridge, and Lawrence). This certainly seems in conflict with Leviticus 18:17-18 and 20:14.[7]

Smith also targeted the young daughters of two of his closest associates. For instance, Joseph Smith attempted to make nineteen-year-old Nancy Rigdon one of his secret plural wives but was soundly rejected. When her father, Sidney, heard of the incident, he confronted Smith. Mormon historian Richard S. Van Wagoner noted how Smith at first denied the story but later admitted it when Nancy did not back away from her accusation. Shortly thereafter Smith had a letter sent to Nancy justifying his proposal when he said, "That which is wrong under one circumstance, may be, and often is, right under another."[8]

In May 1843, the thirty-seven-year-old prophet of Mormonism convinced fifteen-year-old Helen Mar Kimball to be sealed to him as his plural wife. The daughter of Heber C. Kimball stated how Smith promised that if she would "take this step," it would ensure the eternal salvation and exaltation of her father's household and kindred. Helen was led to believe that the relationship was more of a spiritual nature.

---

[6] Ibid., pp. 15-16. Ellipsis mine. Polyandry is one woman marrying multiple men. For a list of Smith's wives and more information, see www.mrm.org/joseph-smith-and-polygamy.
[7] In an article titled "Condemnation and Grace: Polygamy and Concubinage in the Old Testament," Richard M. Davidson argues that the original language in Lev. 18:18 really "refers to any two women, not just to two consanguine sisters." See *Christian Research Journal* Vol. 38 No. 5, 2015, p. 35.
[8] Van Wagoner, *Sidney Rigdon: A Portrait of Religion Excess* (Salt Lake City: Signature Press, 2006), pp. 295-96.

She claimed that she would have never gone through with it had she known otherwise.[9]

Emma, Joseph's first wife, never approved of polygamy. For instance, when Joseph's brother Hyrum took the revelation on plural marriage to Emma in the summer of 1843 to get her permission, he returned with his head down, saying, "I have never received a more severe talking to in my life. Emma is very bitter and full of resentment and anger."[10]

Mormon authors Linda King Newell and Valeen Tippetts Avery explain, "Emma would eventually know about some of Joseph's plural wives, her knowledge of seven can be documented conclusively, and some evidence hints that she may have known of others."[11]

"If Smith's life was not marked by integrity, then the religion he founded ought to be examined with great scrutiny"

Emma was deceived by Smith on a number of occasions. When she found out that certain women—including some of her best friends—were married to her husband, she became angry and even defiant. For instance, "when the full realization of the relationship between her friend Eliza [Snow] and her husband Joseph came to her, Emma was stunned. . . . Although no contemporary account of the incident between Emma and Eliza is available, evidence leads to the conclusion that some sort of physical confrontation occurred between the two women."[12]

While many Mormons remain naïve about the polygamous ways of their church's founder, how could a modern Mormon in good conscience revere someone who lied to his wife about these other relationships while secretly marrying women who were already married to his friends (sometimes without their knowledge)? Any man who is willing to deceive his wife and friends is certainly capable of lying to others.[13]

Speaking at a general conference, Apostle M. Russell Ballard stated that a false prophet was someone who would attempt "to change the God-given and scripturally based doctrines that protect the sanctity of marriage, the divine nature of the family, and the essential doctrine of personal morality."[14]

---

[9] Ibid., pp. 293–94.
[10] Newell and Avery, *Mormon Enigma: Emma Hale Smith* (Chicago: University of Illinois Press, 1994), p. 152.
[11] Ibid., p. 98.
[12] Ibid., p. 134. Ellipsis mine.
[13] Much more can be said about Joseph Smith's questionable behavior. To read more on this topic, check out our website www.JosephsWives.com.
[14] *Ensign*, November 1999, p. 64.

Ballard said such false prophets tend to redefine morality to justify, among other things, adultery and fornication. On such issues Mormons tend to ignore Smith's immoral behavior. Is it not reasonable to expect that the standards given by Ballard should also apply to Smith?

When the history of Joseph Smith is studied, there are too many unanswered questions. This should cause doubt as to whether this man really restored Christianity. If Smith's life was not marked by integrity, then the religion he founded ought to be examined with great scrutiny.

A replica set of the Book of Mormon gold plates that are displayed in the church's history museum in Salt Lake City.

5 Points Overview of Chapter 2

1. Joseph Smith claimed that, in 1820 as a 14-year-old boy, he saw God the Father and Jesus in what Latter-day Saints call the "First Vision."
2. The angel Moroni appeared to Joseph Smith in 1823 and gave him the gold plates containing the Book of Mormon, which he claimed he was able to translate into English from "Reformed Egyptian. The gold plates are said to have been taken back by Moroni and its existence cannot be checked.
3. The church moved to Illinois and the members built a city in the 1840s called Nauvoo.
4. Smith married between 30-40 women, as admitted in an official church essay printed on the lds.org website; a third of these wives were teenagers as young as 14, and another third were already married to living husbands.
5. A mob murdered Joseph Smith at the Carthage Jail in June 1844.

Questions to Ask Your Mormon Friend

In 1978, close to a thousand followers of Jim Jones drank poisoned Kool-Aid and died in the jungles of Guyana. Most did so voluntarily. This catastrophic event took place while I was in high school and caused me great concern when I found out about it. After all, Jones began as a Christian pastor, though he became more crazy as time went on. "How could this have happened?" I asked myself. After all, these people had trusted this man and yet they ended up dying because a false prophet told them to drink cyanide.

Don't get me wrong, as I'm not saying Mormons will commit suicide if they follow Joseph Smith and the Mormon religion. Still, I would bet that most of your Mormon friends only know about the Joseph Smith who is described in their Sunday School and seminary lessons. Few, I have found, know little more than the official version offered by the LDS Church leadership. For instance, your friends may not realize that Smith was a polygamist who married teenagers and other women already married to other men. You might ask,

Does it bother you that Joseph Smith married teenaged girls as young as 14 as well as a mother/daughter and sisters? Or that he married women who were already married to other men?

If they doubt your information, consider taking them to the website JosephsWives.com. While we want to be careful how we approach this sensitive topic, it must be understood that Smith is *not* the saintly example that many Latter-day Saints think he is. The apostle Paul taught how the Christian believer ought to "flee from sexual immorality" (1 Cor. 6:18). He also said that the acts of the sinful nature "are obvious," including "sexual immorality, impurity and debauchery" (Gal. 5:19).

As far as Christian church leaders are concerned, Paul told Timothy that the "overseer must be above reproach, the husband of one wife, sober-minded, self-controlled, respectable ..." (1 Tim. 3:2). From what history has detailed concerning the life of Mormonism's founder, is this really a man whom Christians ought to emulate? Absolutely not!

Your friends may also not know that Joseph Smith regularly contradicted the Bible on important biblical doctrines. If this is the case, should such a teacher be praised? We are commanded to investigate truth carefully and *not* accept false doctrines, even if they are taught by our pastoral leaders. If Joseph Smith taught a different God, a different Jesus, and even a different gospel, why should his teachings be accepted at face value? Encourage your Mormon friend to investigate carefully. Check out Matthew 7:15, Acts 17:11, Galatians 1:8-9, and 1 John 4:1.

Chapter 3: Examining the Attraction of Mormonism

As you read more about Mormonism, it might be hard for you to understand why people would ever want to follow this religion. Like the tides pulled by the moon, so are many who are attracted to the Mormon religion. Let's discuss six of the most common reasons I have found why people decide to convert to Mormonism.

"I grew up in the church"

In the introduction I mentioned how I used to take my students on field trips to the Mormon Battalion Center where the LDS missionaries presented their faith. Sometimes the missionaries used PowerPoint productions, printed outlines, or well-rehearsed talks as part of their presentation. These young men and women were often the best prepared instructors at any religious venue we visited.

There was one thing I could always count on. Unless my memory fails me, each one of the more than two dozen missionaries we encountered at this LDS venue for more than a decade had been born into faithful LDS families. In fact, more than half of the missionary presenters came from predominately Mormon towns in Utah or Idaho. In other words, they had accepted the LDS faith from the cradle. Most likely all of them were baptized at the age of eight and later attended seminary classes in high school before venturing on their missions, using money they had saved for their entire lives.

Of course, there's nothing wrong with believing in a faith taught to us by our families. I would have to say the majority of my high school students grew up in Christian churches in much the same manner. Like many of these missionaries, they had never known anything else. This is why I considered my year-long apologetics Bible course to be so important. "Look to where the facts lead," I taught, "and head in the direction where you find the most reasonable evidence pointing to the truth."

Over and over again I stressed how it was time for these teens to "own their *own* faith" and not borrow someone else's. Instead of believing Christianity as a part of their culture, I wanted my students to believe because Christianity's truth claims best correspond with reality. If my students didn't believe in Christianity by the time they were 16, then they needed to do some research. I even gave them the freedom to disagree with Christianity's claims and write their essays using worldviews different than mine, including atheism. If they didn't accept Christianity, I wanted them to stop pretending that they could be Christians by osmosis.

Many young people are Latter-day Saints because they grew up in this religion and knew nothing else. For them I recommend studying the history and information that is readily available, especially on the Internet. While it is a risky business to look at faiths other than our own, it is important to consider all points of view. The facts should be allowed to be the overriding factor in any decision to determine truth. As Jesus said in John 8:32, it is "the truth (that) will set you free."

"I prayed about the church and know it is true"

Latter-day Saints generally believe their ability to discern doctrinal truth comes through a "personal testimony," which has been called a "burning in the bosom." This term comes from Doctrine and Covenants 9:8, which says,

> But, behold, I say unto you, that you must study it out in your mind; then you must ask me if it be right, and if it is right I will cause that your bosom shall burn within you; therefore, you shall feel that it is right.

One verse in the Bible that may be most often quoted by Mormons (especially the missionaries) is James 1:5 in the New Testament. It says,

> If any of you lacks wisdom, let him ask God, who gives generously to all without reproach, and it will be given him.

Located in the last chapter of the Book of Mormon, Moroni 10:4 is another popular reference. It explains,

> And when ye shall receive these things, I would exhort you that ye would ask God, the Eternal Father, in the name of Christ, if these things are not true; and if ye shall ask with a sincere heart, with real intent, having faith in Christ, he will manifest the truth of it unto you, by the power of the Holy Ghost.

A Latter-day Saint may give you a Book of Mormon and point to this verse. "Pray about this book and see if it's true," the challenge will be made. While it is important to be respectful of our Latter-day Saint friends and not minimize their experiences, explain how the rules have been rigged since the prayer's request has only one correct answer. For those who agree to pray but don't receive the *right* answer, it has been suggested that the potential convert must *not* have a sincere heart, real intent, or adequate faith.

Understand that those who decline to pray (including me) may be asked, "Don't you believe in prayer?" (Answer: *"Of course I do, but prayer needs to be offered in the right way. We are told to 'test the spirits to see if they are from God' (1 John 4:1). Just as I won't pray about whether or not I should steal my neighbor's car, so we shouldn't abuse prayer in an attempt to get a positive feeling about the truthfulness of a religion."*)

When your Mormon friends bring up Moroni 10:4 in a conversation, you might ask whether their feelings have always been accurate. If they are honest, they will admit that, at one time or another, they were fooled, no matter how sincere they were. If this is the case, we must be aware of relying too much on feelings that can possibly mislead us.

For example, Mormons believe that marriage is not only for life but also for eternity. Should it be assumed that the many LDS couples who divorce did not pray about their relationships beforehand? Surely knowing information about another person that could have exposed potential behavior problems—such as drug addiction, personal infidelity, inward apathy to God, or repressed anger—would have helped the person make a more informed decision. Yet how many Mormons "felt" God's approval in relationships that were tragically doomed from the beginning?

What about students who *feel* they have "aced" an exam? Imagine their shock when they see a big fat "F" at the top of their paper, as they missed many more questions than they got right. They thought they *knew* they had this test in the bag, but the facts proved otherwise. Unfortunately, even when confronted with information that is contrary to their belief system, many Mormons remain firm in their faith by clinging to their subjective feelings.

In addition, there are others who belong to other religions and "know" that they are right. Consider how Muslims often testify that "Allah is the only God and Muhammad is his messenger." I have talked to former atheists who claimed how they *knew* that God didn't exist before they became Christians. Just because people have personal testimonies doesn't make their beliefs true. At the same time, please understand that a personal testimony can be a very powerful tool. Telling your story can show others how much your faith means to you. And your conviction may cause the other person to think. Just don't expect anyone to become a Christian based on your testimony alone.

"This church values the family"

Probably nothing is more attractive to potential converts than the family structure promoted in Mormonism. Many activities are meant to bring loved ones together. For example, families are encouraged to meet together for studying scriptural lessons, playing games, and generally having fun on "Family Home Evening," typically held on Monday nights.

In addition, the Mormon community prides itself in taking care of each other. For example, those Latter-day Saints who are struggling or in a difficult situation can participate in the church's welfare program. Emergencies such as medical bills and missed mortgage payments are sometimes covered through the church's welfare system. There is also a "bishop's storehouse" where LDS families can get food items when they do not have enough resources. According to the Bible, Christians are commanded to take care of each other. It is something that many churches do well while others could do even better.

My wife Terri's family

"Mormons aren't hypocritical like those belonging to other churches"

The convictions of most Latter-day Saints lead them to decline offers of drugs or alcohol at a party as well as refusing to participate in premarital sex. Faithful Mormons are even willing to set aside Sundays for church attendance and spiritual reflection, including personal study. Watching football games, going to the store, and doing yard work are activities that are not allowed on the "Sabbath" (Sunday). Some who call themselves "Christian" at your church, school, or neighborhood may not have such high standards, which is something that your Mormon friend may point out.

There is no doubt that many Latter-day Saints are hard-working and do the best they can to observe the teachings of their religion. At the same time, please understand that there are "hypocrites" in every religion, including Mormonism. (If you get to know some Mormons, I'm sure they will admit that there are hypocrites who attend their church's services. If they are honest, they may even admit that they too struggle with hypocritical patterns!) We should be careful *not* to base the truthfulness of a religion on the actions of sinners like you and me. A faith could be true even if there are scoundrels (like me!) who belong to it. It is better to look closely at a faith's claims and line these up with the evidence.

"The Mormon Church has the best answers about life"

Mormonism teaches that it can offer the best answers to the three questions asked by most people: Where did I come from? Why am I here? And where am I going? For the first question, many believe that Mormonism's doctrine of premortality—something not taught in Evangelical Christian churches—is a comforting teaching. However, the idea that a person's behavior in a previous existence (spirit world) is able to have any influence in this life cannot be supported by the Bible.[1] This seems to be more closely aligned to Hinduism's teaching of karma.

As far as the purpose of life, Mormon leaders say the doctrines of their church make the most sense. Their teachings include the necessity of being baptized by those who possess proper authority, the need to be married for both "time" as well as "eternity" in an LDS temple, and the requirement to obey all the commandments. Because they are considered unhealthy based on a doctrine originating from Joseph Smith, hot drinks such as coffee and tea are not allowed. Tithing to the church, which is giving away ten percent of one's income, is a must-do. The hope is that godhood can be attained by keeping commandments.

As we will discuss in the next section, if those who advocate a particular religion end up contradicting the teachings of the Bible, shouldn't this be considered problematic? No matter how sincere a person is, wrong beliefs are never to be considered the "best answers" to life's most important questions and should therefore always be rejected.

"I met a Mormon and love him/her"

Many people joined the Mormon Church because of romance. For example, if a non-member meets a Latter-day Saint, it is a temptation for the person to convert to Mormonism to help make the relationship become permanent. I have known many Christian believers—especially young men—who are willing to leave their old beliefs behind. We will talk about the dangers of Christians dating Latter-day Saints in chapter 8.

---

[1] To read about Mormonism's doctrine of premortality, see chapter 1.

Questions to Ask Your Mormon Friend

My experience has shown me that asking the following question opens many doors. It's quite simple and easy to remember:

Why are you a Latter-day Saint?

This should not be considered an attacking question. By asking it, you have just invited your LDS friends to provide reasons why they believe the way they do. When you ask, hear what they have to say while practicing active listening skills (i.e. looking the other person in the eye, acknowledging the points through your positive body language, and smiling).

Very likely you will be given a testimony that explains how your friend *knows* Joseph Smith is a true prophet of God, how authority has been restored in these "latter days," and how The Church of Jesus Christ of Latter-day Saints is the most correct church on the earth.

On the other hand, Christians are able to base their faith on the Word of God and trust in the work performed by Jesus on the cross for the atonement of their sins. With that in mind, ask your LDS friends how it is possible for them to know whether or not their faith is true. If the facts of the Bible are contradicted—regardless of how many good feelings a person has—then that philosophy or religion needs to be rejected.

There is a follow-up question that ought to also be used in your conversations with the Mormons:

How do you know that?

Become like a police detective who attempts to determine the evidence by asking questions such as these. By doing so, you will learn more about what your friend believes. Be sure to ask in a respectful way so your friend doesn't think you are making personal attacks. Instead of allowing your friends to remain content by trusting in their personal feelings, have them explain to you why they believe the way they do. You might be surprised how little they have critically analyzed their personal belief system.

Small Group Activity

Perhaps you are studying this booklet with another person (or even with a youth group from church). Working with others, I have found, can be a great way to better understand the material presented in a class or book. If this is the case, consider bringing up the following topics to have a group discussion using these ideas to spark the conversation.

1. In your opinion, what are some possible reasons a teenager might want to belong to a certain religion? (i.e. Christian, Mormon, Jehovah's Witness, Muslim, etc.)

Here are some possibilities:

Loyalty to family / heritage
Approval from adults (leaders in the church)
Peer pressure from friends
Ignorance about other possibilities

2. What about you? Why do you hold the faith you do? With that in mind, consider which reason(s) that should be considered valid for permanently holding onto and "owning" your personal faith.

At what age do you think teens begin to think through the different religious possibilities that are out there? (For instance, atheism, Islam, Mormonism, Hinduism, etc.)

3. Should a person seriously research the truth claims of his or her own religion? Why or why not? How would you respond to someone who tells teens not to study other religions because this could be dangerous in possibly making them want to leave their childhood faith?

Should where you are born and how you were raised be the most important factors in how a faith is chosen? Why or why not?

4. Discuss which factors ought to be considered when examining the evidence and determining a faith's truth claims.

How important is a personal testimony of one's faith? If someone asked about your story, how would you respond?

Section 2: The Doctrines of Mormonism

doc·trine
ˈdäktrən/
Noun

a belief or set of beliefs held and taught by a church, political party, or other group.

A Visit to the

If you ever get to Salt Lake City in Utah, I recommend that you check out the Church History Museum (located at 45 N West Temple), just across the street from Temple Square in the Utah state capital city. Admission is free. Among the items you can visit are (clockwise from bottom left):

- a portrait of twelfth LDS President Spencer W. Kimball, with a first-edition copy of The Miracle of Forgiveness displayed in the glass case below (see www.TheMiracleOfForgiveness.com)
- the printing press used to produce the first Book of Mormon copies
- the death mask of Mormonism's founder Joseph Smith
- a picture of a "seer stone" that Joseph Smith claimed he used in the translation of the Book of Mormon—he said that he put the stone in a top hat and the words of the Book of Mormon were shown to him (for more, see www.mrm.org/bom-seer-stone).

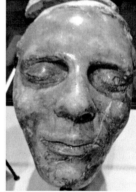

Chapter 4: Examining the God of Mormonism

We have discussed how frustrating it can be when Mormons and Evangelical Christians have conversations involving their faith. What can end up happening is that both sides assume there is agreement when, in reality, there is complete disagreement. Thus, it is important for us to define some of the differences to make sure we are on the same page.

God the Father

According to LDS leaders, the correct version of God is not understood by those outside the Mormon Church. Mormon Apostle Quentin L. Cook wrote, "Among the first principles lost in the Apostasy was an understanding of God the Father."[1] Cook and other leaders suggest that anyone who belongs to a church outside Mormonism cannot properly comprehend God because, it is assumed, the doctrine was changed hundreds of years ago. Apostle Jeffrey R. Holland explained that

> we are very comfortable, frankly, in letting it be known that we do not hold a fourth- or fifth-century, pagan-influenced view of the Godhead, and neither did those first Christian Saints who were eyewitnesses of the living Christ. We are New Testament—*not* Nicene—Christians.[2]

Mormonism teaches that three separate gods exist: God the Father, Jesus Christ, and the Holy Ghost. This is called tri-theism, something much different from the biblical doctrine of the Trinity. While distinct in being, the three gods in Mormonism are considered one in purpose. At the head of the triad is God the Father, who is known as Heavenly Father or Elohim. He was once a righteous human being in another realm who died and then became God of this world. Thus, he had (and still has) a literal body of "flesh and bones." One church manual reports, "His eternal spirit is housed in a tangible body of flesh and bones (see D&C 130:22). God's body, however, is perfected and glorified with a glory beyond all description."[3]

Was God always God? Not according to Mormonism. A church manual explains,

---

Sections from chapters 1, 2, and 3 in *Mormonism 101* were used in this chapter.
[1] Cook, "The Doctrine of the Father," *Ensign*, February 2012, p. 33.
[2] Holland, "Knowing the Godhead," *Ensign*, January 2016, p. 37. Italics his.
[3] *Gospel Principles*, p. 6.

It will help us to remember that our Father in Heaven was once a man who lived on an earth, the same as we do. He became our Father in Heaven by overcoming problems, just as we have to do on this earth.[4]

The teaching that God was once a human being goes back to a sermon given by Joseph Smith in June 1844, just a few days before his death. A Mormon elder by the name of King Follett was "crushed in a well by the falling of a tub of rock." At Follett's funeral, Smith delivered a sermon that became known as the King Follett Discourse. It has been a standard teaching in the church and was reprinted in the May 1971 edition of the official LDS magazine *Ensign*. According to Smith,

It is the first principle of the Gospel to know for a certainty the Character of God. . . . He was once a man like us; . . . God himself, the Father of us all, dwelt on an earth, the same as Jesus Christ himself did.[5]

According to Mormonism, God gradually progressed to the position and power he now holds. President Brigham Young explained,

The doctrine that God was once a man and has progressed to become God is unique to this Church. How do you feel, knowing that God, through His own experience, "knows all that we know regarding the toils [and] sufferings" of mortality?[6]

Contrary to Mormon teaching, the Bible says that there is no fluctuation in God's divine character. There never was a time when God the Father lived "on an earth the same as Jesus Christ did." This is because he *never* was a man who had to progress to become God. In fact, the perfect God of the Bible has no need to change. If He had the ability to better Himself, it would show that He *was* not perfect. Should He make Himself worse, it would show that He *is* not perfect.

As His nature remains constant, so, too, His desires and purposes never change. Speaking about God, the psalmist correctly pointed out how "you are the same, and your years have no end" (Psalm 102:27). In an expression that could not be made any clearer, Malachi 3:6 says, "For I the Lord do not change." James 1:17 adds that "there is no variation or shadow due to change" with the "Father of lights."

---

[4] *Gospel Fundamentals*, p. 7.
[5] *Gospel Principles*, p. 279. Ellipses in original.
[6] *Teachings of Presidents of the Church: Brigham Young*, p. 34.

Although she is not directly mentioned in LDS scripture, Heavenly Mother is assumed to be the wife of God the Father. While Mormon leaders are fairly silent on the doctrine of Heavenly Mother, it is clear that she is not to be worshipped. I use the singular "she," but in fact, there appears to be more than one such being, as earlier LDS leaders taught that God was polygamous with a multiplicity of wives. According to Mormonism, when all the spirits were born in premortality, each had the same Heavenly Father, but there must have been many Heavenly Mothers giving birth to billions of spirits. If this unique LDS teaching is true, the odds are you know nobody who has the same Heavenly Mother as you!

Jesus Christ

The second member of the Godhead is Jesus Christ, God the Father's literal eldest son in premortality. In fact, Jesus and Lucifer are spirit brothers. According to an LDS educator,

> On first hearing, the doctrine that Lucifer and our Lord, Jesus Christ, are brothers may seem surprising to some, especially to those unacquainted with latter-day revelations. But both the scriptures and the prophets affirm that Jesus Christ and Lucifer are indeed offspring of our Heavenly Father and, therefore, spirit brothers. . . . Both Jesus and Lucifer were strong leaders with great knowledge and influence. But as the First-born of the Father, Jesus was Lucifer's older brother.[7]

The Christus statue is located in the North Visitors' Center at Temple Square in Salt Lake City.

Ironically, the same passages of the Bible that expound on Christ's eternal deity also show that Lucifer could not be the brother of Christ. John 1:1–3 says that all things (including Lucifer) were made by Jesus, who was, is, and always will be God. Colossians 1:15, the one biblical reference used by the author above, says, "He (Jesus) is the image of the invisible God, the firstborn of

---

[7] *A Sure Foundation: Answers to Difficult Gospel Questions* (Salt Lake City: Deseret Book, 1988), pp. 223–24. Ellipsis mine.

all creation." As you can look in the mirror and see yourself, so Jesus—as the image of God—can see who He truly is. Verse 17 adds that "he is before all things." If Lucifer had been created by Jesus, how could the two be brothers?

The LDS version of Jesus was not fully God in the beginning and had to "work out his own salvation." Sixth President Joseph F. Smith wrote, "Even Christ himself was not perfect at first; he received not a fulness at first, but he received grace for grace, and he continued to receive more and more until he received a fullness."[8] Apostle Bruce R. McConkie claimed, "Jesus kept the commandments of his Father and thereby worked out his own salvation, and also set an example as to the way and the means whereby all men may be saved."[9] Such teaching is blasphemous and is inconsistent with the Bible, which says Jesus:

- became a man but never lost His deity (Phil. 2:5-7)
- is 100 percent God and 100 percent man[10]
- created the world and everything in it (John 1:3; Col. 1:15-17)
- was conceived through the Holy Spirit (Matt. 1:18–25; Luke 1:35)
- lived a sinless life while being subjected to human temptations (John 5:19; Heb. 2:18; 4:15)
- died a human death before rising again bodily to conquer sin (Rom. 5:6–10; 1 Cor. 15:3–4)
- will return to the earth to judge (John 5:22)
- sent the Holy Spirit to empower believers (John 14–16; Acts 1:8)
- can be prayed to (Acts 7:59)
- deserves honor, love, and worship (Matt. 10:37; John 5:23; 14:1; Heb. 1:6)
- has fullness of deity (Col. 1:19, 2:9) and is our mediator (1 Tim. 2:5)

Just because people say they believe in Jesus is not a guarantee that they have an accurate view of Him. In fact, 2 Corinthians 11:4 says that anyone who preaches "another Jesus" ought to be rejected. A belief in a corrupt Jesus is inadequate and is no better than a denial of the Savior.

Holy Ghost

According to Mormonism, the Holy Ghost is the third member of the Godhead and, like Jesus, is a son of God the Father. However, he

---

[8] *Teachings of Presidents of the Church: Joseph F. Smith*, p. 153. Also see Joseph F. Smith, *Gospel Doctrine*, comp. John A. Widtsoe (Salt Lake City, Utah: Deseret Book Co., 1919), p. 68.
[9] *The Mortal Messiah: From Bethlehem to Calvary* (Salt Lake City: Deseret Book, 2009), 4:434.
[10] Theologians have given this concept a fancy term called the "hypostatic union."

does not have a body. According to Apostle Joseph B. Wirthlin, the Holy Ghost is only present with those who are faithful to Mormon teaching. He said, "When we are confirmed, we are given the *right* to the companionship of the Holy Ghost, but it is a right that we must continue to earn through obedience and worthiness."[11]

The Bible teaches that the Holy Ghost (or Holy Spirit) is the third Person of the Trinity. Christianity teaches that when someone becomes a believer in Christ, there is a special indwelling called the baptism of the Spirit. This Helper, as He is called, makes it possible for the believer to better understand God and His ways (1 Cor. 2:10-12).

The Trinity

Joseph Smith said that "when I have preached on the subject of the Deity, it has been the plurality of Gods." He ridiculed the Trinity:

> It is a curious organization. . . . All are to be crammed into one God, according to sectarianism. It would make the biggest God in all the world. He would be a wonderfully big God—he would be a giant or a monster.[12]

Mormon Apostle Jeffrey R. Holland asked:

> How are we to trust, love, and worship, to say nothing of striving to be like, One who is incomprehensible and unknowable? . . . So we are very comfortable, frankly, in letting it be known that we do not hold a fourth– or fifth-century, pagan-influenced view of the Godhead. . . .[13]

Christian apologist James White defines this vital doctrine:

> Within the one Being that is God, there exists eternally three coequal and coeternal persons, namely, the Father, the Son, and the Holy Spirit.[14]

In the early church, the biblical doctrines were challenged, compelling the leaders to answer the heretical charges being raised. Contrary to LDS belief, the Trinity (the Latin terms "Tri" and "Unity" put together) is not a philosophical invention; rather, it explains the biblical position of Christianity.

---

[11] "The Unspeakable Gift," *Liahona*, May 2003, p. 27. Italics in original.
[12] Joseph Fielding Smith, ed., Teachings of the Prophet Joseph Smith (edited by Joseph Fielding Smith), pp. 370, 372. Ellipsis mine.
[13] "Knowing the Godhead," *Ensign*, January 2016, p. 37. Ellipses mine.
[14] James White, *The Forgotten Trinity: Recovering the Heart of Christian Belief* (Minneapolis: Bethany House Publishers, 1998), p. 26.

Over and over again the Bible emphasizes the importance of the belief in only one true God. This was a major point of separation between the religious system of the Jews and their pagan neighbors. This pattern is found throughout the Old Testament. When God rejected King David's offer to build Him a house, the humble king prayed and said, "There is none like you, O Lord, and there is no God besides you, according to all that we have heard with our ears (1 Chron. 17:20).

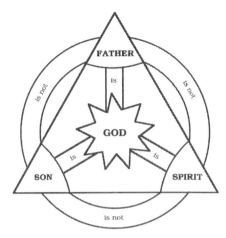

This type of illustration was used in the early Christian church to explain the Trinity.

The Old Testament book of Isaiah offers support to the defense of monotheism—the belief and worship of only one God—than any other. Throughout chapters 43 through 45, Isaiah emphasized the existence of one God alone. For instance, Isaiah 43:10 says that no gods exist before or after the one true God of Israel; Isaiah 44:6 and 8 say that God doesn't know of other true gods. Wouldn't it be strange if the omniscient God of the universe didn't realize that He once lived under the rule of another god? Is He really ignorant of the fact that His children have the ability to become gods in their own right?

The existence of one God is confirmed in the New Testament as well. Deuteronomy 6:4 says, "Hear, O Israel: The Lord our God is one Lord," which Jesus cited to an inquiring Jewish scribe. In response, this scribe remarked in Mark 12:32, "You are right, Teacher. You have truly said that he is one, and there is no other besides him." Notice how Jesus responded in verse 34: "You are not far from the kingdom of God."

Each member of the Trinity is separate in Personhood from the other members. Each Person—being fully, one hundred percent God in His own right—is *not* identical to the others. For example, Jesus was fully God in the very beginning. Thomas called Him both "Lord" and "God" (John 20:28). And Jesus claimed that, while He was not the Father, He came as God in the flesh who "dwelled" among humanity.

Some skeptics argue that Jesus appears to be lesser in being than the Father. For example, John 14:28 may be cited ("for the Father is greater than I") to show how Jesus is not God. However, Jesus was referring to a *position* of authority and not His nature. Just as your teachers are "greater" than you and the principal is "greater" than they, so too is the Father greater than Jesus. Equal in nature yet lesser in authority.

A Mormon may wonder about Jesus's prayer to the Father in the Garden of Gethsemane. "Was Jesus a ventriloquist who prayed to himself?" you may get asked. Point out that the Trinity does not teach that the Father is Jesus or that Jesus is the Holy Spirit. There are three Persons in the Trinity; thus, there is communication within the Godhead. If one member of the Trinity communicates with another, this does not negate the deity of either one. Jesus was *not* a ventriloquist; instead, He was praying in the Garden of Gethsemane to the Father, the One to whom Jesus subjected Himself. The Father and the Son are *not* the same person.

I don't have room here to give a thorough study on this very important issue. Just understand that the Trinity—though a mystery—explains how there can be three Persons (Father, Son, and Holy Spirit) who are all God, yet there is only one God. Most well-meaning illustrations (such as the egg or water) logically break down, but I have found one to be useful. Ask your friend, "What does one and one and one equal?" Most likely the answer will be "three." This is true when the three numbers are added together. Yet when the three numbers are multiplied (1 x 1 x 1), the answer is still 1!

If it can be demonstrated that the Father, Son, and Holy Ghost/Spirit are God, and at the same time it can be shown that there is only one God, it would definitely jeopardize an important Mormon teaching.[14]

5 Points Overview of Chapter 4

1. God the Father in Mormonism once lived as a man.
2. The LDS version of Jesus says that Jesus is a created god and is lesser in nature than the Father.
3. The Bible is adamant that there is only one God in existence and that there can be no gods existing before or after Him.
4. Mormonism teaches that there are three separate gods in the Godhead: the Father, Son, and Holy Ghost.
5. The Trinity, a vital Christian teaching, is rejected by Mormons.

---

[14] For a series of articles on the Trinity, go to www.mrm.org/trinity-index.

Questions to Ask Your Mormon Friend

A famous couplet by fifth President Lorenzo Snow states, "As man is, God once was. As God is, man may become." (Most likely your Mormon friend has heard this before.) Although some may say that this statement gets into some pretty deep theology, we need to determine just what Mormonism teaches about God and see how this doctrine might differ from biblical Christianity. According to Mormonism:

- God has not always been God
- He became God through obedience in a previous earth-like existence
- He still exists in a body of flesh and bones and is a resurrected being (D&C 130:22)
- Humans living in this world have the potential to attain godhood (in their own right) in the same way that God was able to become a god
- Families can live together forever based on successfully keeping *all* of the commandments continually (D&C 25:15-16)

Using Snow's couplet, ask your Mormon friend the following:

Do you believe God the Father was once a human? If he was, did He have a God before Him? And how did He become God?

While your friend may say God's origin is difficult to understand, the Bible is adamant that God has always been God (Psalm 90:2). He does not have a body of flesh and bone, but He is spirit and must be worshipped "in spirit and in truth" (John 4:24). In addition, there is no god before or after the true God of the Bible, as stated in Isaiah 43:10. God says that He doesn't even know of any other gods, a strange admission if multiple gods do exist.

In this chapter, Apostle Holland explained that he was unable to "trust, love, and worship" an incomprehensible God. Yet LDS leaders often deflect questions about the origin of the Mormon God because it too is incomprehensible. It seems like a double standard. And we would agree that just because a concept is beyond our thoughts, this doesn't negate the existence of that concept.

Biblical References You Can Use When Sharing Your Faith

Witnessing:

> **Proverbs 12:15; 28:26:** Only fools trust in feelings
> **Proverbs 14:12, Jeremiah 17:9:** Don't trust in feelings
> **2 Corinthians 11:4:** False Christs do exist
> **Galatians 1:8-9:** False Gospels do exist
> **Ephesians 4:15:** Speak the truth in love
> **1 Thessalonians 5:21:** Test everything
> **1 Peter 3:15-16:** Share the truth in gentleness/respect
> **1 John 4:1:** Test spirits to see if they are from God
> **Jude 3:** Contend for the Christian faith

Godhead:

> **Deuteronomy 6:4; Mark 12:29:** God is one God
> **Psalm 90:2:** God is God from eternity to all eternity
> **Isaiah 43:10:** No God before or after God
> **Isaiah 44:6, 8:** God knows of no other gods
> **Malachi 3:6:** God does not change
> **John 1:1-3, 14; 8:58 (with Ex. 3:14); 10:30; 20:28; Phil. 2:5-11; Col. 1:15-17, 2:9:** Jesus is God
> **John 4:24:** God is Spirit (He must be worshipped in truth!)
> **1 Corinthians 15:1-5:** The resurrection of Jesus is true

Salvation:

> **Matthew 1:21:** Jesus came to save His people from sin
> **John 1:12; Rom. 8:14; 9:8:** Children of God come by faith
> **John 6:47:** He who believes in Jesus has eternal life
> **John 14:6; Acts 4:12:** Salvation found only in the true Jesus
> **Acts 16:31:** Believe in Jesus and you will be saved
> **Romans 3:23:** All are sinners/fallen short of God's glory
> **Romans 3:28; Gal. 2:15-16:** Justified by faith, not law
> **Ephesians 2:8-9:** Salvation comes by grace through faith
> **Titus 3:5-6:** Salvation comes by God's mercy
> **1 John 5:13:** It is possible to know if you have eternal life

Chapter 5: Examining the Scriptures of Mormonism

According to Mormon teaching, there are four written scriptures that are authoritative: the Bible, the Book of Mormon, the Doctrine and Covenants, and the Pearl of Great Price. Together these are called the Standard Works. Let's take a look at each of these important LDS scriptures.

The Bible (King James Version)

The Bible is a best-selling book that is accepted by Christians as the authoritative Word of God. Faithful Christian missionaries throughout the world work overtime translating this book into new languages. While Christians uphold the Bible as the sole written authority for Christ's church, many Mormons have criticized this scripture despite the fact that it is a part of their Standard Works.

For example, some will claim that the Bible has been changed over the years. The Book of Mormon states in 1 Nephi 13:28, "Wherefore, thou seest that after the book hath gone forth through the hands of the great and abominable church, that there are many plain and precious things taken away from the book, which is the book of the Lamb of God." Second Nephi 29:6 adds, "Thou fool, that shall say: A Bible, we have got a Bible, and we need no more Bible. Have ye obtained a Bible save it were by the Jews?"

Officially, Mormons use the King James Version of the Bible.[1] The eighth Article of Faith, which was written by Joseph Smith in 1842, says that the Bible can be trusted only "as far as it is translated correctly." What does this mean? *Translation* means to take words from one language and put them into the words of another language. If the Bible is true only as far as it is *translated* correctly, we would certainly agree. In this context, however, it appears that the word *translated* really means *transmitted*. Unfortunately, those who mistakenly think that the Bible cannot be trusted apparently do not understand how the Bible's manuscripts have been preserved since New Testament times.

Christian theologian Ron Rhodes lists some of the incredible statistics of the manuscript support for the Bible:

Sections from chapters 7-9 in *Mormonism 101* were used in this chapter.

[1] I have often wondered if the LDS Church leaders have continued to use this hard-to-understand-in-the-21st-century translation because they know how difficult it is for their followers to understand. I have met many former Latter-day Saints who ended up leaving Mormonism once they understood the concepts taught in the Bible.

> There are more than 24,000 partial and complete manuscript copies of the New Testament. . . . There are also some 86,000 quotations from the early church fathers and several thousand Lectionaries (church-service books containing Scripture quotations used in the early centuries of Christianity). . . . The Dead Sea Scrolls prove the accuracy of the transmission of the [Old Testament]. In fact, in these scrolls discovered at Qumran in 1947, we have Old Testament manuscripts that date about a thousand years earlier (150 B.C.) than the other Old Testament manuscripts then in our possession (which [are] dated to A.D. 900). The significant thing is that when one compares the two sets of manuscripts, it is clear that they are essentially the same, with very few changes. The fact that manuscripts separated by a thousand years are essentially the same indicates the incredible accuracy of the Old Testament's manuscript transmission.[2]

The Bible was written primarily in Hebrew and Koiné Greek. Any time the words from one language are put into another—whether it is Spanish into English or French into Arabic—there is the risk of losing something in the translation. It is doubtful that most modern-day translations were produced by evil people who wanted to keep God's truths hidden. In actuality, quite the opposite is true. The motivation behind a new English translation is, in most cases, to give a clearer understanding of what God wants to reveal to His people, though it is true that some translations do a better job at achieving this goal than others.

Although they will differ, a good translation goes back to the most accurate biblical manuscripts and then attempts to put the words into an understandable language for the audience it addresses. Two translators of any written piece will differ in the choice of words, verb tense, and style. But if two good Spanish translators independently translate a history textbook, the basic message would most likely be the same despite the numerous differences in vocabulary and sentence structure. In fact, there can be no such thing as a *perfect* translation. The LDS Church leaders must certainly be aware of this, since their translators have often had to revise not only their English edition of the Book of Mormon but several foreign editions as well.

The Book of Mormon

Although many might think it is nothing more than the name of a Broadway musical, the Book of Mormon is the scripture that your

---

[2] http://home.earthlink.net/~ronrhodes/Manuscript.html. Ellipses added.

friends may ask you to read for yourself. Written in King James English, it is said to contain the story of two groups of people who came to the Americas. The first group was known as the Jaredites. The *Encyclopedia of Mormonism* describes their history:

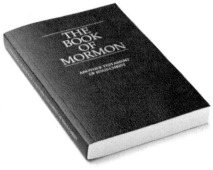

> This particular people left the Tower of Babel at the time of the confusion of tongues. Their prophet-leaders were led to the ocean, where they constructed eight peculiar barges. These were driven by the wind across the waters to America, where the Jaredites became a large and powerful nation. After many centuries, wickedness and wars led to a final war of annihilation. During that final war, Ether, a prophet of God, wrote their history and spiritual experiences on twenty-four gold plates, perhaps relying on earlier Jaredite records.[3]

The second group arrived in the Americas approximately six hundred years before the birth of Jesus. Lehi, a Jewish prophet from Jerusalem, claimed that God told him to leave the city prior to the Babylonian captivity in 586 B.C. He fled with his wife, Sariah, and their four sons: Laman, Lemuel, Sam, and Nephi. Also joining Lehi were Zoram, Ishmael, and Ishmael's family. They sailed across the ocean, landed in the Western Hemisphere, and eventually built cities and a large civilization. After Lehi's death, some of the people accepted Nephi as their leader, while the rest gave their allegiance to Laman.

The Book of Mormon narrative describes how these two groups were known as Nephites and Lamanites. Much of the story is based on the hatred between the two groups, resulting in a number of wars. The LDS scripture also records Jesus's appearance to these civilizations after he was resurrected from the dead in Palestine. By the fifth century A.D., the Lamanites had completely destroyed the Nephite people at the battle of the Hill Cumorah.

According to Mormonism, the descendants of the Lamanites are the Native Americans. Moroni, who was the son of Mormon, was the last living Nephite. He buried the record of his people in the Hill Cumorah, which is located near present-day Palmyra in upstate New York. This record on gold plates was given to Joseph Smith; according to Mormon leaders, this translation is the Book of Mormon.

---

[3] Ludlow, ed., *Encyclopedia of Mormonism,* vol. 1, s.v. "Book of Mormon plates and records," p. 200.

While most LDS scholars believe that there is historical and scientific value in the Book of Mormon, there appears to be no scientist or historian outside the Mormon faith who supports such a notion. On August 25, 1984, scientist John Carlson noted, "The Book of Mormon itself has not made a significant contribution to New World archaeology. Ask any New World archaeologist."

Dr. Michael D. Coe, a non-Mormon professor emeritus of anthropology at Yale University, is an expert in the early history of Mesoamerica. He wrote a paper in 1973 that discussed the lack of historical evidence in the Book of Mormon. Said Coe:

> Mormon archaeologists over the years have almost unanimously accepted the Book of Mormon as an accurate, historical account of the New World peoples between about 2000 B.C. and A.D. 421. They believe that Smith could translate hieroglyphs, whether "Reformed Egyptian" or ancient American. . . . Let me now state uncategorically that as far as I know there is not one professionally trained archaeologist, who is not a Mormon, who sees any scientific justification for believing the foregoing to be true, and I would like to state that there are quite a few Mormon archaeologists who join this group. . . . The bare facts of the matter are that nothing, absolutely nothing, has ever shown up in any New World excavation which would suggest to a dispassionate observer that the Book of Mormon, as claimed by Joseph Smith, is a historical document relating to the history of the early migrants to our hemisphere.[4]

In a PBS television documentary broadcast in 2007, Coe stated:

> In the case of the Book of Mormon, you've got a much bigger problem. You really do. We have another part of the world where the archaeology is really very well-known now; we know a lot about people like the Maya and their predecessors. So to try to find unlikely evidence in an unlikely spot, you've got a problem. And of course none of the finds that biblical archaeologists are rightly proud about, no finds on that level have ever come up for Mormon archaeologists, which makes it a big problem.[5]

---

[4] "Mormons and Archaeology: An Outside View," *Dialogue* 8 (Summer 1973): pp. 41, 42, 46. Ellipses mine.
[5] www.pbs.org/mormons/interviews/coe.html

The Doctrine and Covenants

A church article reported, "We testify that the Doctrine and Covenants is truly the Lord's voice in our time to each child of God and that great blessings come to those who study it."[6] According to the explanatory introduction to the Doctrine and Covenants (D&C):

> The Doctrine and Covenants is a collection of divine revelations and inspired declarations. . . . Although most of the sections are directed to members of The Church of Jesus Christ of Latter-day Saints, the messages, warnings, and exhortations are for the benefit of all mankind. . . . [It] is unique because it is not a translation of an ancient document, but is of modern origin and was given of God through his chosen prophets for the restoration of his holy work and the establishment of the kingdom of God on the earth in these days.

Three of the more important doctrines recorded in the D&C include:

- the Word of Wisdom, a health code that, when obeyed, brings "temporal and spiritual blessings" (Section 89)
- baptism for the dead that should be performed in LDS temples (Sections 124, 127, 128)
- God has a body of flesh and bone and, along with Jesus, may make appearances to men (Section 130).

In addition, the D&C contains two "Official Declarations," the first given in 1890 that officially banned plural marriages, and the second given in 1978 that allowed for all worthy male members, including blacks, to hold the priesthood.

Most of the D&C was authored by Joseph Smith who claimed he was prompted to write down revelations from God. Mormons must take Smith's word that he actually heard from God and wrote down modern-day revelation. Since much of what has been recorded is contrary to the Bible, the D&C—along with the other unique LDS scriptures—is not authoritative for Bible-believing Christians.

The Pearl of Great Price

According to the introductory note found in this scripture:

---

[6] "Enriching Your Study of the Doctrine and Covenants," *Ensign*, January 2009, p. 47.

The Pearl of Great Price is a selection of choice materials touching many significant aspects of the faith and doctrine. . . . These items were produced by the Prophet Joseph Smith and were published in the Church periodicals of his day.

Apostle Franklin D. Richards put the first collection of materials together in 1851. Over the years revisions were made, including sections that were taken out of the Pearl of Great Price in 1979 and moved to the D&C (Sections 137 and 138). It has five parts:

1. **Selections from the Book of Moses**. This was taken from the Old Testament book of Genesis. It is often quoted in the notes to the LDS-published Bible as well as church magazines and manuals.
2. **Joseph Smith—Matthew**. A one-chapter reinterpretation of Matthew 23:39 and chapter 24.
3. **Joseph Smith—History**. Includes "excerpts from Joseph Smith's official testimony and history, which he prepared in 1838 . . ."
4. **The Articles of Faith**. Written by Smith and originally known as the Wentworth Letter, these are the thirteen major points of LDS doctrine.
5. **The Book of Abraham**. Using Egyptian papyri, Joseph Smith made a translation into English and published it in the *Times and Seasons* publication beginning in 1842. It is said to contain "priceless information about the gospel, pre-existence, the nature of Deity, the creation, and priesthood, information which is not otherwise available in any other revelation now extant."[7]

Just like what must be done with the D&C, Mormons must place their complete trust in Joseph Smith in order to accept the authenticity of the Pearl of Great Price. Yet there are problems with what is written in this unique LDS scripture. Smith claimed that the writing on the papyrus he had purchased from an entrepreneur traveling through Ohio in 1835 originated from the Old Testament patriarch Abraham. Egyptian hieroglyphics could not be deciphered in America during the time of Smith. The papyrus was later discovered in the Metropolitan Museum in New York during the mid-1960s and, according to contemporary Egyptologists, contains nothing more than common Egyptian funerary writings. Dr. Robert K. Ritter, a professor of Egyptology at the University of Chicago, explained:

> I want to be absolutely clear on this. There simply is no justification for the kind of interpretations that appear in facsimile one or facsimile three. They are wrong with regard to

---

[7] Bruce R. McConkie, *Mormon Doctrine* (Salt Lake City: Bookcraft, 1966), p. 564.

the hieroglyphs, they are wrong with regard to the gender, they are wrong with regard to the understanding of what the scene actually represents and where they are used in the body of the text. They are wrong there as well. In short, there is no historical validity for the interpretations in that book [the Book of Abraham]. None whatsoever.[8]

Revelation 22:18

Some Christians may attempt to use Revelation 22:18 ("I warn everyone who hears the words of the prophecy of this book: if anyone adds to them, God will add to him the plagues described in this book") to show how these LDS scriptures are unacceptable. However, this is an improper use of this verse, as it is only talking about the book of Revelation, not the whole Bible.

It is not necessary to use a particular verse to reject the unique LDS scriptures. Christians don't accept these other scriptures (the Book of Mormon, Doctrine and Covenants, and Pearl of Great Price) because they cannot be verified through archaeological or historical evidence as support. Therefore, these books are rejected.

For instance, it cannot be historically or scientifically verified that ancient Israelites ever lived on the American continent. The idea that Joseph Smith had the ability to translate Egyptian hieroglyphics is very doubtful. It must be taken on faith alone that Joseph Smith had personal contact with God, allowing him to write down "modern-day revelation" as supposedly revealed in the D&C, especially since much of the teaching found in this unique LDS scripture contradicts the doctrines of the Bible. Thus, we must not take this biblical verse out of context to make it say something that was never intended.

5 Points Overview of Chapter 5

1. Mormonism teaches that the King James Version of the Bible is true, but only as far as it is "translated correctly."
2. Your friends may try to get you to read the Book of Mormon, a scripture that is supposed to describe ancient Jews in the Americas, and then have you pray about it to see if it's true.
3. Most LDS doctrine comes from the Doctrine and Covenants.
4. The Pearl of Great Price includes miscellaneous writings, including the Book of Abraham, Joseph Smith-History, and a retranslated portion of the gospel of Matthew.
5. The teachings of church leaders are also considered scripture.

---

[8] Check out an hour-long documentary on YouTube: https://www.youtube.com/watch?v=hcyzkd_m6KE or type "Book of Abraham full movie" into YouTube's search engine.

Questions to Ask Your Mormon Friend

As I wrote in this chapter, your Mormon friend may challenge you to read the Book of Mormon. This is something you should consider. If you do decide to read this unique LDS scripture, perhaps having a parent or trusted friend join you would be helpful. Highlight verses (many seem contradictory to Mormonism) and write down questions as you read.

Here are some possible questions you can ask:

- I noticed that many of these events were supposed to have taken place during biblical days. We have archaeological evidence to help us see that many people, places, and events discussed in the Bible are real. Could you please point me to any evidence to show that these events discussed in the Book of Mormon are historical?
- Joseph Smith once said that the Book of Mormon was the "most correct book on earth" and that a person could better understand God through this book. What are some of the things I can find in this book that weren't previously discussed in the Bible?
- Moroni 10:4 says that it is possible to pray with "true intent" and a "sincere heart" and the rad can know the Book of Mormon is true. While I believe in prayer, does God command that we should determine truth with prayer? After all, aren't many sincere in their belief that the Aur'an is true and Muhammad is God's prophet?

When you receive an invitation to read Book of Mormon, perhaps you should challenge your Mormon friends to read a modern version of the Bible. For example, suggest having them read one of the New Testament gospels or a Pauline epistle. Ask,

"If I gave you a modern version of the New Testament, would you be willing to read it?"

Explain that a modern Bible version uses modernl language much easier to understand than the King James Version that was originally translated in 1611. A good translation will be faithful to the meaning of the original Hebrew (Old Testament) and Greek (New Testament) used in the Bible. If your friend is willing, ask your parents or pastor for a copy of a modern version that you can give away.

Maybe you would even be willing to read the book of John with them. Other wonderful New Testament books that could spark a variety of conversations include Romans, Galatians, and Ephesians. Remember, the Bible is Mormon scripture too! Imagine how many spiritual conversations could take place. Let God's Word speak for itself. Many ex-Mormons who became Christians did so after accepting this challenge.

Chapter 6: Examining the Salvation of Mormonism

Atonement	The sacrifice Jesus made in the Garden of Gethsemane and on the cross, allowing a person to overcome sin, adversity, and death.
Commandments	Rules of living as taught in Mormonism.
Covenants	Promises made to God at baptism and confirmation, the weekly sacrament, temple endowment, and temple marriage (sealing), all of which are crucial for exaltation.
Exaltation	Synonymous with eternal life, the status given to those who qualify for godhood.
Gift of the Holy Ghost	Fullness of blessings available to LDS members. The Holy Ghost stays with only those who keep commandments.
Gospel	All doctrines, principles, laws, ordinances, and covenants required to receive exaltation.
Ordinance	Ceremony in which the Mormon makes covenants with God. It includes baptism, sacrament, and work in the temple.
Repentance	The process by which members receive forgiveness and feels sorrow for their sins.
Salvation (General and Individual)	Depending on the context, this could refer to general salvation (general resurrection for all humans) or individual exaltation (available only to those who are obedient).

Say the words "saved by grace" or "the **atonement**" to a Latter-day Saint and you are likely to get a positive reaction because they have important meaning. Do these words mean the same as what is understood by Bible-believing Christians?

In Mormonism, the word "salvation" is divided into two categories. First, there is **general salvation**, which is resurrection provided to all people regardless of their faith or obedience. Grace is bestowed on all humans since they chose wisely in premortality, giving them physical bodies necessary to progress to the next life. This is known as "resurrection from the dead." Based on the work done by Jesus at both

---

Sections from chapter 11 in *Mormonism 101* were used in this chapter.

Gethsemane as well as the cross, all humans will be eligible for one of three kingdoms. There is also **individual salvation**, which is eternal life earned by faithful Mormons who keep all of God's commandments. In order to attain the top level of heaven, known as the celestial kingdom, a person must become a member of the Mormon Church, repent, and keep the **commandments**. This, in a nutshell, is the Mormon **gospel**.

Requirements for Exaltation

Unlike resurrection from the dead, **exaltation** requires an individual to live according to all of Mormonism's commandments. A person must participate in **ordinances**, including being water baptized at a Mormon chapel as well as being confirmed and receiving the **Gift of the Holy Ghost**. Those who hope to attain the celestial kingdom are expected to overcome all sins and live righteously. In a 2012 general conference talk, Seventy Robert C. Gay stated:

> This is the exchange the Savior is asking of us: we are to give up all our sins, big or small, for the Father's reward of eternal life. We are to forget self-justifying stories, excuses, rationalizations, defense mechanisms, procrastinations, appearances, personal pride, judgmental thoughts, and doing things our way. We are to separate ourselves from all worldliness and take upon us the image of God in our countenances.[1]

Mormons can never have full assurance that all their sins are forgiven, as twelfth President Spencer W. Kimball explained:

> It is true that many Latter-day Saints, having been baptized and confirmed members of the Church, and some even having received their endowments and having been married and sealed in the holy temple, have felt that they were thus guaranteed the blessings of exaltation and eternal life. But this is not so. There are two basic requirements every soul must fulfill or he cannot attain to the great blessings offered. He *must* receive the ordinances and he *must* be faithful, overcoming his weaknesses. Hence, not all who claim to be Latter-day Saints will be exalted.[2]

Over and over again, LDS Church leaders have stated that, by itself, God's grace—though necessary for the "atonement"—cannot fully "save" people from their sins. Doctrine and Covenants 25:15 says, "Keep my commandments continually, and a crown of righteousness

---

[1] "What Shall a Man Give in Exchange for His Soul?" *Ensign*, November 2012, p. 35.
[2] *Teachings of Presidents of the Church: Spencer W. Kimball* (Salt Lake City: The Church of Jesus Christ of Latter-day Saints, 2006), p. 9. Italics in original.

thou shalt receive. And except thou do this, where I am you cannot come." As Henry B. Eyring, a member of the First Presidency, put it, "To receive the gift of living with Him forever in families in the celestial kingdom, we must be able to live the laws of that kingdom (see D&C 88:22). He has given us commandments in this life to help us develop that capacity."[3]

Faithful Mormons make promises to keep the commandments of God at baptism, in the temple, and each week at the Sunday church service when they take the sacrament. In a straightforward address given in the *Ensign* magazine titled "Understanding our Covenants with God," the leaders stated:

> A covenant is a two-way promise, the conditions of which are set by God. When we enter into a covenant with God, we promise to keep those conditions. He promises us certain blessings in return. When we receive these saving ordinances and keep the associated covenants, the Atonement of Jesus Christ becomes effective in our lives, and we can receive the great blessing God can give us—eternal life (see D&C 14:7). Because keeping our covenants is essential to our happiness now and to eventually receiving eternal life, it is important to understand what we have promised our Heavenly Father.[4]

Latter-day Saints are not supposed to postpone keeping the promises they make to God. Their accomplishments are supposed to take place in this life and *not* the next. This teaching is made very clear throughout the standard works as well as the teachings of the leadership in their writings along with what has been written in church manuals and magazines. For instance, Kimball stated:

> Only as we overcome shall we become perfect and move toward godhood. As I have indicated previously, the time to do this is *now,* in mortality. Someone once said: "A fellow who is planning to reform is one step behind. He ought to quit planning and get on with the job. *Today* is the day."[5]

When confronted with the fact that they cannot keep all of the commandments, many Mormons find comfort in their ability to repent. Admitting to their sins through **repentance**, they think, erases the transgression and makes everything all right. Such an attitude that repentance can fix the sin problem is certainly frowned upon by the church's leaders. Instead, "abandonment of sin" is continually stressed: "although confes-

---

[3] *Ensign*, June 2011, p. 4.
[4] *Ensign*, July 2012, p. 22.
[5] *The Miracle of Forgiveness* (Salt Lake City: Deseret Book, 1969), p. 210. Italics mine.

sion is an essential element of repentance, it is not enough. The Lord has said, 'By this ye may know if a man repenteth of his sins—behold, he will confess them and forsake them' (D&C 58:43)."[6] Using this verse, a popular church manual states,

> Our sincere sorrow should lead us to forsake (stop) our sins. If we have stolen something, we will steal no more. If we have lied, we will lie no more. If we have committed adultery, we will stop.[7]

Kimball said, "The forsaking of sin must be a permanent one. True repentance does not permit making the same mistake again."[8] This idea is emphasized in an LDS student manual:

> **D&C 58:42–43. The Lord Promises Complete Forgiveness to Those Who Truly Repent.** The Lord forgives those who truly repent of their sins. This blessing comes through the Atonement of Christ, who "suffered . . . for all, that they might not suffer if they would repent" (D&C 19:16). The Lord promises that He will no more remember the sins of those who repent (see Ezekiel 18:21–22). Repentance, however, requires that we forsake and turn completely from our sins and confess them.[9]

Another verse that ought to greatly concern the Latter-day Saint is D&C 82:7. It says, "And now, verily I say unto you, I, the Lord, will not lay any sin to your charge; go your ways and sin no more; but unto that soul who sinneth shall the former sins return, saith the Lord your God." A church resource manual provides guidance for the teacher:

> **Doctrine and Covenants 82:7. We are commanded to forsake sin. If we sin again after repenting, our former sins return. (5–10 minutes)** Bring several rocks to class that are all labeled with the same sin (for example, breaking the Word of Wisdom). Tell students a story about an imaginary person who commits this sin. Invent details to

---

[6] *True to the Faith: A Gospel Reference* (Salt Lake City: Intellectual Reserve, 2004), p. 134.
[7] *Gospel Principles* (Salt Lake City: The Church of Jesus Christ of Latter-day Saints, 2009), p. 110. Parenthesis in original.
[8] Kimball, *Repentance Brings Forgiveness*, an unnumbered tract. *Doctrine and Covenants Student Manual Religion 324 and 325* (Salt Lake City: Intellectual Reserve, 2001), p. 122. Boldface and ellipsis in original.
[9] *Doctrine and Covenants Student Manual Religion 324 and 325* (Salt Lake City: Intellectual Reserve, 2001), p. 122. Bold and ellipsis in original.

embellish your story. Each time the imaginary person commits the sin, pick up a rock, until you are holding several of them. Set all the rocks you are holding aside and ask: • What might setting the rocks aside represent? (Repentance.) • What happens to our sins when we repent? (The Lord forgives them.) Read Doctrine and Covenants 82:7 and look for what happens when we sin again. Ask: • How many rocks would a person need to pick up if he sins after repenting? (All that you were previously holding plus a new one.) • Why do you think our former sins return? • What does that teach you about the importance of forsaking sin? • How can knowing this doctrine help you avoid sin?[10]

There is no doubt that, according to Mormonism, keeping commandments after repentance is not just a suggestion but is an absolute requirement. Quoting D&C 1:31, a reference handbook states,

> The Lord has said that He "cannot look upon sin with the least degree of allowance" (D&C 1:31). The result of sin is the withdrawal of the Holy Ghost and, in eternity, being unable to dwell in the presence of our Heavenly Father, for "no unclean thing can dwell with God" (1 Nephi 10:21).[11]

Referring to this same D&C passage, Kimball—who had claimed that "perfection is an achievable goal" [12]—wrote:

> This scripture is most precise. First, one repents. Having gained that ground he then must live the commandments of the Lord to retain his vantage point. This is necessary to secure complete forgiveness.[13]

Kimball also said that the "repentance which merits forgiveness" is where a person reaches a "point of no return" and have

> a deep abhorrence of the sin—where the sin becomes most distasteful to him and where the desire or urge to sin is cleared out of his life.[14]

---

[10] *Doctrine and Covenants and Church History Seminary Teacher Resource Manual* (Salt Lake City: Intellectual Reserve, 2013), p. 134. Bold in original.
[11] *True to the Faith: A Gospel Reference*, p. 163.
[12] Kimball, *The Miracle of Forgiveness*, p. 170.
[13] *Teachings of Presidents of the Church: Spencer W. Kimball*, p. 43. Ibid. See also the First Presidency Message in the March 1982 *Ensign* magazine titled "God Will Forgive."
[14] *The Miracle of Forgiveness*, p. 355.

Apparently many Mormons are apparently not doing this, according to Apostle Richard G. Scott:

> Time and time again at funerals, statements are made that the deceased will inherit all blessings of celestial glory when that individual has in no way qualified by obtaining the necessary ordinances and by keeping the required covenants. That won't happen. Such blessings can only be earned by meeting the Lord's requirements. His mercy does not overcome the requirements of His law. **They must be met.**[15]

Salvation according to Christianity

Unlike most of the other chapters of this book, great stress has been given in this chapter to quoting multiple LDS sources, both general authorities of the LDS Church and the official manuals. It doesn't get much more authoritative than that! Many other citations are available to show how successfully forsaking sin is necessary for a hope of qualifying for Mormonism's exaltation.[16] Let's be honest, nobody has been successful in permanently ending sin; it was Jesus who, while we were still sinners, died on the cross as payment in full for those who accepted His free offer (Rom. 5:8).

It is impossible to consistently obey God's commandments. Not even the apostle Paul believed he had ever reached this state, as he explained in Romans 7:15 and 18-20:

> For I do not understand my own actions. For I do not do what I want, but I do the very thing I hate. . . . For I know that nothing good dwells in me, that is, in my flesh. For I have the desire to do what is right, but not the ability to carry it out. For I do not do the good I want, but the evil I do not want is what I keep on doing. Now if I do what I do not want, it is no longer I who do it, but sin that dwells within me.

When it comes to salvation, the message of Christianity differs from what is taught in Mormonism. When people accept Jesus Christ as their Lord and Savior, a miraculous event occurs. They are made right (justified) by God Himself and are thereby declared guiltless, allowing them to be identified with Christ from the point of conversion to eternity future. It does not come by a person's own efforts but by God's work in that person. The New Testament contains many exam-

---

[15] "First Things First," *Ensign* (Conference Edition), May 2001, p. 9. Emphasis mine.
[16] To see more on this topic, go to http://www.mrm.org/salvation.

ples of how faith, not obedience of the commandments, makes people clean in God's sight and forgives them from all sin:

- Jesus said in John 5:24 that "whoever hears my word and believes him who sent me has eternal life. He does not come into judgment, but has passed from death to life."
- He also said in John 6:47 that "whoever believes has eternal life."
- Acts 13:39 says it is "by him everyone who believes is freed from everything from which you could not be freed by the law of Moses."
- Philippians 3:9 explains how salvation did not come by "having a righteousness of my own that comes from the law, but that which comes through faith in Christ, the righteousness from God that depends on faith."
- Romans 5:1 states, "Therefore being justified by faith, we have peace with God through our Lord Jesus Christ."
- Ephesians 2:8–9 says faith, not works, justifies a person before God.
- Titus 3:5–6 explains how Christians are saved "not because of works done by us in righteousness, but according to his own mercy, by the washing of regeneration and renewal of the Holy Spirit, whom he poured out on us richly through Jesus Christ our Savior."

Since sinful humans are unable to comply with God's standards,[17] they deserve death. After all, good works, by themselves, are like "polluted garments" ("filthy rags" says the King James Version) in God's sight.[18] It is through faith that believers are able to experience the fellowship of God and have all sins forgiven.

Do good works matter to a Christian?

Your Mormon friend may be quick to reference James 2:14–26 in an attempt to show how "faith without works is dead." If faith alone is all that is needed for "salvation," as the argument goes, then it would seem reasonable that Christians could do whatever they willed (i.e., murder, commit adultery, steal) and still call themselves Christians.

Christians, however, agree that "faith without works is dead." In fact, the Christian church has *never* taught that the believer is free to break God's commands. Paul explained in Romans 6:15, "What then? Are we to sin because we are not under law but under grace? By no means!" As needs to be done with every passage, the context of James chapter 2 should be understood. Written by the half-brother of Jesus to explain how good works *are* important, James did not teach that Christians receive salvation through works. Rather, his point was to show how good works would accompany a valid salvation.

---

[17] See, for instance, Rom. 3:23; Gen. 8:21; Ps 51:5, 58:3; Eccles. 9:3; Jer. 17:9.
[18] Rom. 6:23; Isa. 64:6.

Perhaps a favorite illustration that I regularly use in my evangelism encounters will make the point. Imagine a young man whose family and friends are in attendance at his 16th birthday party. The boy opens a card given to him by Grandpa: "Dear Grandson, I love you," it says. "I have put 10 into the bank for your birthday. Enjoy it. Love, Grandpa."

An ungrateful teenager may be lacking in appreciation for the grandfather's gift. (Of course, you know better, right?!) After all, a measly 10 bucks might make it appear that Grandpa—who isn't poor—is not very generous. Suppose this young man tosses the card aside with hardly a thought. However, the time will come when this teen could use a few extra dollars, such as today when he needs gas for his car. Driving around town, the boy decides to stop by the bank and collect his money. Let's go to the scene.

The young man walks up to the teller and gives her his ATM card. She looks at the computer screen, types on her keyboard, and then gives him a receipt along with a crisp new $10 bill. As he merrily walks out the door, imagine his disgust when he looks at the paper and realizes how a huge joke has just been played on him. He storms back to the teller, knocking into the customer at her window while raising his voice and exclaiming, "How dare you! What a terrible hoax!"

The teller looks at him, befuddled. "What are you talking about?" He glares. Then, holding out the crumpled bank receipt, he exclaims, "Why did you make the computer say I have $9,999,990?" Looking firmly at him, she responds, "Well, you took out $10. Take that away from the $10,000,000 in your account, and this is what you have left."

What do you think the boy will do when he realizes how his grandfather gave him $10,000,000, not $10? After all, this is more money than 90% of all Americans will ever earn in a lifetime of work. (A person would have to earn $200,000 a year from the ages of 18 to 68 to equal this incredible amount of money!) Would his attitude be one of anger toward his grandfather or of deep love and appreciation?

If the young man has any sense, he would choose the latter attitude. A normal human being would not desire to throw lye on his grandfather's grass, kick his dog, and spray graffiti on the garage door as a response to this lavish gift. At the very least, a thank you card is in order. (Did your parents make you write these after every birthday and Christmas?) No, this would

Illustration purchased through Fotosearch

seem to require much more. Indeed, the young man decides to drive to his grandfather's home to thank him in person.

Upon arrival, though, he sees the six-inch high grass in his grandfather's yard. When he understands that the gardener had to be let go because Grandpa didn't have any money left over, the boy decides to get the lawnmower out of the shed and mow Grandpa's grass. You know what? It feels good to do something nice for somebody who has made such a huge sacrifice for you. In fact, suppose the grandson decides it feels so good that he comes back week after week to mow the grass. It is

> "It's not a matter of how often the man-made rules of Mormonism are kept that gives a person the ability to claim forgiveness from sin"

the least he could do, he thinks to himself. And it brings such joy to his grandfather.

At the end of the year, would this same grandson have any right to suggest that he had "paid back" Grandpa after a year of mowing the grass? Hardly. The money was a gift; it was never intended to be repaid. Mowing the grass shouldn't have been considered a requirement to earn the $10 million gift. (Consider that doing this every week for 40 years—52 weeks a year—would result in 2,080 visits, the same as $4,800 per mowing. If only you could get such a job!)

Just a verse after Ephesians 2:9 says that the Christian is "saved by grace through faith" and not "by works," Paul continues in verse 10 by saying how the believer is "God's workmanship" who is "created for good works" before he or she was ever born. The apostle is certainly not contradicting what he had just written; rather, he is showing how good works ought to be a part of a believer's life, even a natural reaction when the cost of grace so freely provided is understood.

It's not a matter of how often the man-made rules of Mormonism are kept that gives a person the ability to claim forgiveness from sin. Instead of tossing the birthday card aside, a truth seeker ought to consider picking up the Bible to see what God's love letter is all about. When the gift of eternal life is accepted, there will be a natural desire to please God. Good works, which are also known as the fruit of the spirit, will follow. But there cannot be enough good works to ever *earn* the gift.

Galatians 5:4 says, "You are severed from Christ, you who would be justified by the law; you have fallen away from grace." Whether this involves physical circumcision, dietary law, or going to church each

Sunday, keeping numerous rules and regulations will never help a person attain the peace that passes all understanding that is offered by God (Phil. 4:7).

If you are a Christian who has accepted Jesus as your Lord and Savior, you can be eternally grateful to God that you "may know that you have eternal life" (1 John 5:13). What a glorious promise! What a glorious hope!

5 Points Overview of Chapter 6

1. In Mormonism, everyone receives a "general" salvation, allowing humans to attain one of three eternal kingdoms.
2. The gospel of Mormonism requires the adherent to obey all commandments as dictated by the LDS Church for any chance to attain the celestial kingdom.
3. A Mormon must get water baptized, attend church services, and get married in the temple for time and eternity, among many other requirements, if there is to be a chance at eternal life, which is also known as exaltation.
4. LDS scripture stresses how true repentance results in the person not doing that sin ever again.
5. Christianity teaches in salvation by grace through faith alone and that good works are done as a result of true faith; they can never justify a person before God.

Questions to Ask Your Mormon Friend

Those who think that it is possible to earn God's mercy are trusting in themselves for salvation. All other religions outside of Christianity require much to have a chance at eternal life. Consider:

- Muslims practice the five Pillars of Faith, including praying five times a day and fasting during the month of Ramadan. Paradise awaits those whose good works outweigh the bad.
- Buddhists must meditate regularly to reach Nirvana, which has been likened to the extinguishing of a lit candle.
- Hare Krishna devotees recite the "maha mantra" hundreds of times each day and abstain from eating meat, among other requirements.

Unlike these other works-based religions that ask "What must we do for God," Christianity asks "What did God do for me?" The Bible says that nobody could ever be good enough to earn eternal life. Jesus came to this earth to provide His people with the gift of eternal life.

Like other world religions, Mormonism demands obedience from its followers. With your understanding that the word "salvation" contains nuances not easily detected by the language alone, ask your Mormon friend,

> *In your opinion, what must I do to get the very best your religion (Mormonism) has to offer?*

Of course, eternal life, or exaltation, is going to the celestial kingdom. Allow your friend to name some things that they think must be done. They will likely reference getting baptized in the LDS Church, getting married for time and eternity in a Mormon temple, and keeping commandments until the end of time You may also be told about how important it is to attend church services and observe the Sabbath as well as not drinking alcohol or hot drinks. When they are done listing requirements, ask, "Are you doing everything you're supposed to be doing?"

Most Mormons respond by saying that they are doing the best they can or even *trying* hard to do everything that is commanded. As this chapter has explained, complete effort while falling short of the goal is not good enough. The honest Latter-day Saints who do not do what their leaders have continually taught should have great concern for their spiritual welfare. As a Christian, you have the truth. Share it![19]

---

[19] To learn more about how to become a Christian based on the teaching of the Bible, see Appendix 2. You can also visit www.mrm.org/become-a-christian.

Archaeology and the Bible

Biblical archaeology provides credibility for the Bible. Yes, faith is still required, but there is plenty of evidence to support the existence of peoples, events, and places mentioned in the Bible. Evidence for the Book of Mormon people and places does not exist, meaning this scripture's truthfulness must be accepted on faith alone. I have led more than 350 people (including more than 100 high school students) to the Holy Land on nine different occasions since 2009. It is awesome to experience these biblical sites!

Above: The old city of Jerusalem, with the Western Wall in the middle of the picture. This is the holiest place for Jews today, many of whom come here to pray. Above on the hill is the Islamic Dome of the Rock, which is Islam's third holiest site. This structure stands atop the place where the temple's Holy of Holies was located

Middle left: "Jacob's Well," which was used by Jacob and the Samaritan woman in John 4. The well is located in a church basement in ancient Sychar near Samaria. Visitors are invited to drink the cold water from this deep well!

Bottom left: Archaeologist Joel Kramer explains how the walls of Jericho fell down. Type "Joel Kramer Jericho" into the search engine of YouTube to watch several videos that I have produced on this topic.

Photos by Eric Johnson.

Part III: The Relationships in Mormonism

re·la·tion·ship
rəˈlāSH(ə)nˌSHip/
noun

the way in which two or more concepts, objects, or people are connected, or the state of being connected

Taking a visit to

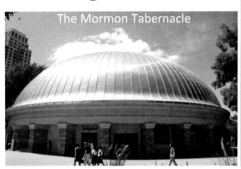
The Mormon Tabernacle

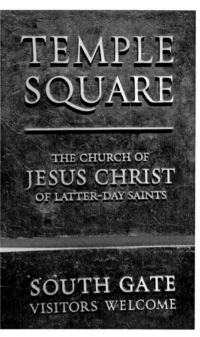
TEMPLE SQUARE
THE CHURCH OF JESUS CHRIST OF LATTER-DAY SAINTS
SOUTH GATE VISITORS WELCOME

A place to check out the next time you're in Utah is Temple Square in downtown Salt Lake City, the top tourist attraction in the state. It's a great place to talk to missionaries and hear the LDS perspective.

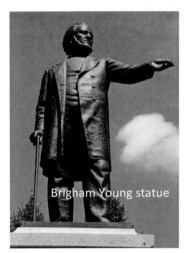
Brigham Young statue

The Salt Lake Temple (seen from the South Visitors' Center)

The Beehive House

Chapter 7: Examining the Educational System of Mormonism

Baptism for the Dead	A rite taking place in a Mormon temple whereby the participant is literally immersed in a baptismal font in the place of someone who has passed away.
Bishop	A man who leads a branch or ward, similar to a Christian pastor. He volunteers his time and is usually employed outside the LDS Church.
Born in the Covenant	The birth of a child to parents who were sealed for both "time" and "eternity" in an LDS temple links this child to the parents in eternity.
Branch	A group of church members in a town or city (not enough to be a ward) that gathers together each Sunday.
Chapel	The main sanctuary of a meetinghouse where members gather each week for the sacrament meeting. Sometimes this is synonymous with "meetinghouse."
CTR	A Mormon youth slogan meaning "Choose the Right."
Endowment Ceremony	Course of instruction for the patrons given in an LDS temple.
Fast and Testimony Sunday	During the first weekend of the month, members are supposed to not eat two meals. The money they would have spent on food is then donated to a church fund intended for needy members. Instead of a message in the sacrament meeting, several members take turns on the first Sunday of each month "bearing their testimonies."
Institute	A class held in a building near a college campus covering information related to Mormonism.
Meetinghouse	A building used for meetings throughout the week, including regular church services. It usually contains offices, a baptismal font area, a kitchen, and a cultural hall. Sometimes the building is referred to as a chapel.
Mutual	Midweek meetings for Latter-day Saints ages 12-17.

Patron	A person who participates in a temple ceremony.
Proxy	Work in the temple done on behalf of those already dead.
Priesthood Meeting	Males 12 or older participate in Aaronic and Melchizedek meetings each Sunday.
Primary	Children ages 3-11 attend special Sunday services where they learn Bible and Book of Mormon stories.
Relief Society Meeting	A class held each Sunday for women who are 18 years of age or older.
Sacrament Meeting	A service that takes place each Sunday in all branches and wards. Each meeting includes hymns, prayers, and a message along with the passing of the sacrament.
Seminary	A daily class held in a church building near a high school covering LDS scripture and history.
Stake	A group of five or more branches or wards are combined to form a stake.
Stake President	The man who leads a particular stake.
Temples	Special buildings found throughout the world where "sacred" rites take place. Mormon youth under the age of 18 are encouraged to regularly attend the temple so they can participate in baptism for the dead.
Temple Recommend	An ID card for Mormons who use the temple. Church commandments must be kept, including not having sex outside marriage, not drinking coffee or tea, and regularly attending church services.
Ward	A group of 150-500 church members living in the same area that meets each Sunday at a local meetinghouse. Mormons in a certain area belong to a particular ward.
Washing/ Anointing	A special temple ceremony where workers symbolically wash and bless body parts of a patron before the patron is anointed with olive oil.
Young Women's Meeting	A class held each Sunday for girls between the ages of 12-17.

Education from the youngest ages through adulthood is considered to be a priority in the Mormon religion. Let's begin with the makeup of the local church body. A group of 150-500 individuals (with a minimum of 15 active Melchizedek priesthood holders) makes up a **ward**; in the United States and Canada, a minimum of 300 people are required. If a town or city doesn't have enough members to make up a ward, the gathering is called a **branch**.

Believers who live in a specific area belong to a particular ward. This is why the Mormon friends in your particular neighborhood all attend the same building, which is called a **chapel** or **meetinghouse**. Five or more wards are combined into what is called a **stake**.

Leaders of the local believers include a **bishop** who volunteers his time and serves the local congregation, much like a Christian pastor or priest. A **stake president** is in charge of the stake. In highly populated areas where there are many Mormons—for instance, in Utah and Idaho—multiple congregations may meet at the same chapel during different times of the day.[1]

The average meetinghouse includes classrooms, offices, a baptismal font, and a kitchen. Many meetinghouses have a cultural hall, sometimes with a stage that can be used for drama or music programs. Basketball hoops that can be lowered for games are featured in many cultural halls. This area is often located in the back half of the meetinghouse's chapel, which is used each Sunday for the **sacrament meeting**—normally during the first hour. It may also be the overflow room for the Sunday meeting.

Everyone attends the service, including infants and toddlers. For those who are not used to distractions, it might seem strange to see babies or fussy toddlers remaining in the service; since Mormon families tend to have more children than not, it's just part of the make-up of a typical Sunday service. Members will sing hymns from a special LDS hymnal while one or more speakers will offer prayers, give announcements, and present a message during the hour-long service that is usually led by the bishop. If you live in a place with a high LDS population (i.e. Utah, Idaho, and even Arizona), the chances are that more than one ward shares the meetinghouse. Meetings are therefore staggered to accommodate several congregations.

Each week members participate in the sacrament, which is very similar to Christianity's communion or Lord's Supper observance. The elements for the sacrament are bread and water, which are offered to church members. This is one of the times where covenants with God are made. If you ever attend a service, I recommend politely declining the

---

[1] Even if several wards are located at the same chapel, the LDS buildings seem to be located on almost every corner in highly populated LDS communities. For instance, according to a September 2014 article in the *Salt Lake Tribune,* there is one chapel every 1.4 square miles in Salt Lake County. Sometimes two chapels are located next to each other!

elements as they come by while remaining respectful during this time.

The first Sunday of each month is called **Fast and Testimony Sunday**. Members are encouraged to skip two consecutive meals and donate the savings to a special church fund. During the service, members are invited to come to the front and "bear their testimonies" about how they *know* Joseph Smith is a true prophet, how the current prophet holds the keys to salvation, and how the Mormon Church is true.

There are two additional hours where members separate and go to different meetings. Young children ages 18 months to three years of age attend nursery. Children ages 3 to 11 go to **primary**. Lessons are typically based on Bible and Book of Mormon stories; all LDS children from around the world receive the same lesson.

There are different Sunday School classes for members 12 and older. For one of the hours, members break up into male and female groups. For girls who are 12 to 17, there is a **Young Women's meeting**. For women 18 or older, there is the **Relief Society meeting**. There are both Aaronic and Melchizedek **priesthood meetings** for the males who are 12 or older.

The same teaching material for these meetings is used in all LDS services throughout the world. Each year members study one of the church's scriptures (Bible, Book of Mormon, Doctrine and Covenants, or the Pearl of Great Price). On the second and third Sundays, members read and discuss a church manual. Beginning in 1998, a different manual has been printed every year (or, twice, every two years) so the members can study a particular president's writings and teachings. The book is titled *Teachings of Presidents of the Church*.[2] In addition, two years were dedicated to studying the 2009 church manual *Gospel Principles*.

What if I'm invited to attend an LDS church service?

Every meetinghouse has a sign outside that reads "Visitors Welcome." (Unlike the information provided on signs located outside many Christian churches, service times for Mormon services are not posted!) A Mormon friend may invite you to come to a Sunday morning service. If your parents think this is OK, it can become an educational opportunity. If you are curious and decide to attend, I recommend going on the first Sunday of the month to observe members' testimonies in the service. Hearing personal stories of the Mormons can be interesting.

To show respect, I encourage you to wear nice clothes, as wearing anything casual may be considered disrespectful. The Mormon boys and men will typically wear white shirts and ties with a dark pair of slacks and black shoes. Meanwhile, girls and women usually wear dresses or blouses and skirts. Females who come a Sunday service in pants are considered to be rebellious by some Mormons.

---

[2] Check out a series of reviews I have written on the manuals printed since 2012: www.mrm.org/teachings-of-presidents-topics.

As a visitor, you should realize that you may be watched very closely by those in regular attendance. One of my daughters attended a "mission send-off" at a local chapel that honored one of her school friends who was departing for his mission. Because she was wearing a cross necklace, she was taken aside by a Mormon acquaintance and told how rude she was. My daughter explained that she didn't intend to offend anyone but that the cross was a very important symbol to her.

If you do attend a service, here are some points to consider:

- Be polite and don't interrupt the service.
- Be a good witness and listen to what is being said.
- Think about the differences between what your friend is learning and what you believe is true.
- If you are invited to share during the Sunday School time, consider asking questions. Most likely your Mormon friend and others are curious what you think about their church or what is being taught. By asking questions, you can clarify what your friends believe, even if it differs from official church teaching.
- Use the experience to have a quality discussion at a later time with your friends about their beliefs.

There are certain things that Latter-day Saints are not supposed to do on Sundays, including doing any yard work, playing games, watching TV, going to movie theaters, and shopping at stores. Thus, if you wanted to work on a school project or go fishing with Mormon friends on a Sunday, they may not be available to do so.

Another meeting that you may get invited to is when a Mormon missionary candidate is sent off to a particular state or country. Boys are able to become missionaries at the age of 18 (for 2 years) while females can go staring at 19 (for 18 months). It is traditional for Mormon families to gather together to watch the candidate open up the letter from the LDS Church announcing the city/country where that individual will be sent. (Deep down, most faithful LDS youth hope to be sent to an exotic, out-of-country destination rather than Utah or another place where Mormonism is common.) There will also be a special service for the missionary just before being sent off to the mission field.

You may be asked to attend one or both of these events. Should you? There are two differing opinions:

1. Some feel that attending these events equals approval of the Mormon religion. By trying to show support of your friend, could your attendance be misunderstood as agreeing with the Mormon religion?

2. Others feel that, because these events are so important to the Mormons, a Christian who doesn't attend without having a good excuse will be considered rude. Shouldn't the relationship be more important than possibly being misunderstood?

Personally, I lean toward option 1, as I think having anyone believe you're in approval of Mormonism by attending these events is a possible drawback. While we are certainly commanded to love our Mormon friends, I hope the message we send in our relationships with them is that truth matters. If the others who see you in attendance think it means that you have no problem with Mormonism, they might not be challenged to think through the important issues, including doctrinal differences as addressed in Section 2 of this book.

My two youngest daughters have practiced the second option, something that their mother and I have allowed them to do. They feel that their relationships mean more than the principle advocated by the first choice. More than three-quarters of their high school friends were LDS. My daughters sometimes used the invitation to give their missionary friends handwritten letters describing their beliefs about Christianity along with an explanation about why they disagree with Mormonism. At the same time, they let the friend know how much they cared for him or her, which is epitomized in their attendance. As a father, I considered this to be a reasonable compromise. All in all, this is a personal issue that ought to be determined by each individual child in conjunction with the parents.[3]

Youth Educational Opportunities

There are other educational opportunities for Latter-day Saint young people. One is called **mutual**, which is a mid-week meeting for Latter-day Saints ages 12 through 17. Boys who turn 12 have the opportunity to become Aaronic Priesthood holders, providing them special privileges and opportunities to serve in the church, including participating in serving the sacrament.

High school students (grades 9-12) are invited to enroll in **seminary** classes that regularly meet throughout the school year at a nearby church building. In highly populated Mormon areas, there is usually a seminary building located next door to the high school. In Utah, public schools "release" those students who want to attend the seminary during the school day. It is treated as a class period for the school; other students will attend classes before or after school. These sessions—

---

[3] In 1 Corinthians 8 and 10, Paul talks about the issue of eating meat offered to idols. Is it OK to eat such meat? Paul answers "yes" and "no." Yes, if it doesn't harm your conscience. No, if it conflicts with the conscience of a weaker brother (1 Cor. 8:9). Using these points for guidance, Christians must make wise decisions with the freedom they have been given.

taught by an LDS teacher—cover Mormon scripture, history, and doctrine.

A popular 44-page booklet that the youth are encouraged to read is titled *For the Strength of Youth*, which was published in 2011. Along with some doctrinal issues, the booklet covers topics such as dating, dress and appearance, entertainment and the media, music and dancing, and sexual purity.[4] For many years, Latter-day Saint youth have worn **CTR** rings and bracelets to remind them to obey the commandments. The letters CTR stand for "Choose the Right"—it comes from an LDS hymn and has been trademarked by the Intellectual Reserve, an LDS Church-owned company.

There are also one-week overnight summer sessions called "Especially for Youth" that are held throughout the western United States and sponsored by Brigham Young University. Students are encouraged to interact with teens outside their own area and learn how to "strengthen their commitments to the gospel of Jesus Christ."

For those who attend colleges and universities, **institute** classes are available. What happens here is similar to the seminary. These classes are held in buildings owned by the LDS Church, usually in close proximity to the college campus.

The Temple

The LDS Church owns special buildings throughout the world called **temples**.[5] According to Mormonism, attending the temple—known as the "House of the Lord"—is important for eternal life, or exaltation. Unlike the chapels where regular services take place, temples are reserved for "sacred" work to be performed by **patrons**. They are open Mondays through Saturdays but closed on Sundays since what takes place in the temple is considered to be work.

To become qualified to enter a temple, candidates must be interviewed by the local leaders who ask questions about their personal conduct. The candidate must be sexually pure and abstain from drugs or alcohol as well as "hot" drinks such as tea or coffee. They also must give ten percent of their income ("tithe") to the LDS Church. Those who are approved are given a **temple recommend**, which is a special identification card allowing entrance to any LDS temple for two years. Nobody is allowed to enter the temple without this card, even those who attend church services regularly.

Adults go through the temple as couples. Each patron first participates in a **washing and anointing** ceremony, getting individually blessed by a temple worker. From here, patrons participate in the **en-**

---

[4] For a review that I wrote on this publication, go to www.mrm.org/strength-of-youth.
[5] As of June 2019, there are 162 operating LDS temples in the world, with several dozen more planned to be built and others scheduled to be remodeled. The number of temples has more than tripled in just two decades when, in 1996, there were only 49 LDS temples.

dowment ceremony where they learn about the creation of the world and the events in the Garden of Eden. In the next room they are given a "new name," which is needed in the next life to "pass through a curtain, known as a "veil"; these names are confidential and can only be known by that person and his/her spouse. The couple also learns special handshakes—known as "tokens"—that will be required for entering the celestial kingdom. When they are finished, the patrons pass through a curtain and enter into the "celestial room," which is symbolic of life in the celestial kingdom. It is here, Mormons believe, that they can be reunited with their families to live forever.

Couples attend the temple just once for themselves. After this, they are encouraged to attend regularly in order to participate in **proxy** work on behalf of those who have already died. Mormons perform genealogical work by researching their family histories so that their relatives who are already deceased may have a chance to hear the Mormon gospel.

Those children born to a temple-married couple are considered **born in the covenant,** which auto-

Salt Lake Temple

matically seals them to their parents forever. For those parents who convert to Mormonism after their children are born, a special ceremony can take place with the parents and the children in a temple that seals them together. It should be pointed out, however, that each member of the family must qualify for the celestial kingdom on their own through individual obedience; nobody is allowed entrance to this state by this sealing alone.

While young teens will have to wait until they are older to have access to all temple activities, they are allowed to participate in **baptisms for the dead**. A baptismal font located at the bottom level of the temple resembles a large hot tub; this is positioned on the back of twelve oxen (symbolizing the Old Testament tribes of Israel).

Based on its name, some may falsely assume that what takes place here must somehow involve a dead person being taken out of the coffin and placed into the font. This, fortunately, is not the case! Instead, a Mormon wearing special clothing goes into the font and is baptized by proxy for each name that is called. Many Mormon youth groups even take group field trips to be immersed for those whom they believe are waiting in spirit prison, a temporary holding place after death, so these souls can be visited by spirit missionaries.

You should also know that those who attend the temple are required to wear special undergarments with unique markings as a reminder about covenants made in the temple; in addition, many consider these garments as a protection from physical and spiritual harm. While your friends may not wear these, their parents may. Finally, while you may find the temple and the ceremonies to be interesting, your Mormon friends are not supposed to talk about specific things taking place in this building. Thus, it is considered rude to ask specific questions about temple activity.

In case you were wondering, visitors are never admitted. The only time non-Mormons can go inside a temple is when one is newly built or an older temple is rededicated. When this happens, there is typically a three- or four-week "open house" event for the public. Once the event is done, the doors will be closed to temple recommend-holding members only. If you get a chance to visit a temple's open house event—an average of two to four of these events are held each year in cities throughout the United States—you may want to go. Just understand that if you sign any visitor cards at the end of the tour, you may be contacted later. If you and your parents think that this is OK, then fill out the card.[6]

The Role of the Temple in the Bible

There are many differences between the temples of Mormonism and the temple of Jerusalem. For example, only one temple was allowed in biblical times while there are dozens of LDS temples throughout the world. In addition, there were no marriage ceremonies or "new names" given in the biblical temple. Most of what took place in the temple of the Bible involved the slaughter of animals for the forgiveness of sins.

Following Jesus's death and resurrection, Jewish temple worship lost its significance with His followers, as a new covenant was established. Hebrews 8:12–13 states,

> For I will be merciful toward their iniquities, and I will remember their sins no more. In speaking of a new covenant, he makes the first one obsolete. And what is becoming obsolete

---

[6] Check out a newspaper that we like to give away outside some temple open house events by clicking a PDF link at the top of the site sacredorsecret.com.

and growing old is ready to vanish away.

Hebrews 9:11-15 shows how the old system no longer is needed:

> But when Christ appeared as a high priest of the good things that have come, then through the greater and more perfect tent (not made with hands, that is, not of this creation) he entered once for all into the holy places, not by means of the blood of goats and calves but by means of his own blood, thus securing an eternal redemption. For if the blood of goats and bulls, and the sprinkling of defiled persons with the ashes of a heifer, sanctify for the purification of the flesh, how much more will the blood of Christ, who through the eternal Spirit offered himself without blemish to God, purify our conscience from dead works to serve the living God. Therefore he is the mediator of a new covenant.

Because of the work done by Jesus on behalf of His people, there is no need today for animal sacrifices today. Temple work was fulfilled through the sacrifice of Jesus on the cross. What takes place in Mormon temples has no biblical precedence, as these human regulations were never intended by God. In essence, Mormonism has added to the gospel of biblical grace.

5 Points Overview of Chapter 7

1. Mormons attend regular church services each Sunday at their ward or branch.
2. These services last three hours every week.
3. Educational opportunities abound in the Mormon Church.
4. Mormon temples allow qualified Latter-day Saints to do work on behalf of both the living and the dead.
5. The LDS temple rituals are different from Bible times.

Questions to Ask your Mormon Friend

Our goal in talking about the important (though sensitive) topic of Mormonism is not to "bash" or "trash talk" any individual who believes in Mormonism. As mentioned in the introduction, we intend to have conversations with "gentleness and respect." At the same time, this issue is very important and we don't want to pretend that differences between our faiths don't exist.

There may come a time when your Mormon friend asks you to come to church. If this happens, it could be a wonderful opportunity. But place a challenge to your Mormon friend as well. A possible response:

> *"You know, I've always wanted a chance to visit your church. Let me ask my parents if that would be OK. And if I go to your service, would you be willing to come with me to my church service one Sunday?"*

You may feel uncomfortable going to an LDS service, and that's perfectly understandable. Or it might not be something your parents want you to do. If this is the case, then politely decline.

But, if you and your parents are agreeable, this could be a chance to experience each other's place of worship and possibly bring up more conversations about important faith matters. If you do attend, be aware of what is happening around you while you remain very respectful. How does the LDS service compare to yours? Try to determine why they do things the way they do. Write down your questions during the service and class and be sure to listen to those things that are said.

If your friend comes to your service, explain the reasons why your church does things the way it does. If there is a worship band, for instance, it may be a new experience for your friend, as only hymns are sung in LDS services. The goal in these interactions is to encourage friendly dialogue that provides the chance to discuss important issues. I consider this to be a possible educational opportunity for everyone involved.

Quick Quiz on Mormonism

Based on what you have learned so far, are you able to answer the following questions? (Forgive me, but I can't help giving a quiz since I'm a teacher at heart!)

1. The founder of this religion is:
   - A) Brigham Young
   - B) Joseph Smith
   - C) John Smith
   - D) Spencer Kimball

2. The name of this church is:
   - A) The Church of Jesus Christ
   - B) The Church of the Latter-days
   - C) The Church of Jesus Christ in the Latter-days
   - D) The Church of Jesus Christ of Latter-day Saints

3. Which is NOT true concerning Mormonism's view of God?
   - A) He has always been God
   - B) He can be prayed to
   - C) He has a physical body
   - D) Called Heavenly Father

4. The idea that Christianity (and its authority) died soon after the death of the Apostles, requiring a "restoration," is called:
   - A) Outer Darkness
   - B) Judgement Day
   - C) Great Apostasy
   - D) Falling Away

5. The very best a Mormon hopes to get by keeping commandments and "enduring to the end" would be this kingdom where one hopes to attain godhood.
   - A) Telestial Kingdom
   - B) Terrestrial Kingdom
   - C) Outer darkness
   - D) Celestial Kingdom

6. Your LDS high school friends can attend the temple and participate in this very important temple ordinance:
   - A) Baptisms for the dead
   - B) Sealing for the dead
   - C) Washing and anointing
   - D) Sitting in the celestial room

7. In which of the following LDS scriptures can you find the story of ancient Americans and a visit to the people from Jesus?
   - A) Bible
   - B) Book of Mormon
   - C) Doctrine and Covenants
   - D) Pearl of Great Price

1. B   2. D   3. A   4. C   5. D   6. A   7. B

Chapter 8: Examining the Dating System of Mormonism

Mormonism teaches that it is possible for faithful church members to get married for "time" only if they get married outside the temple. However, marriage for "time and eternity" is a union that will last beyond death; this "sealing" can take place only inside the temple. With this as a background, let's consider the wisdom of a Christian getting romantically involved with a Mormon or, for that matter, anyone who doesn't hold to a biblical faith.

Dating Outside the Faith

In earlier days, LDS leaders discouraged church members from dating non-Mormons. For example, Apostle Mark E. Petersen wrote a fictional book that portrayed a conversation between a young Mormon girl and her mother about a non-Mormon boy whom she was casually dating. Responding to the daughter's question, "Are other people's ideas of God so different?" the mother answered,

> Yes, very different. You do not know much about other peoples' religions because you have never attended any other church. But there are some so-called Christian churches which do not believe in God as a person at all. They think he is an essence, like an invisible cloud with no shape or substance, and that he is everywhere at once, yet in no place in particular. . . . Many teach that God has neither body, parts, nor passions, which of course is the same as saying that he is not a person at all, but just some indefinable influence and yet so small it can dwell in your heart. Can you see that you and Bob probably don't even worship the same God?[1]

Like Petersen, twelfth President Spencer W. Kimball commanded LDS Church members *not* to date nonmembers. He wrote,

> Clearly, right marriage begins with right dating. . . . Do not take the chance of dating nonmembers, or members who are untrained and faithless. A girl may say, "Oh, I do not intend to marry this person. It is just a 'fun' date." But one cannot afford to take a chance on falling in love with someone who may never accept the gospel.[2]

Sections from chapter 12 of *Answering Mormons' Questions* were used in this chapter.
[1] Mark E. Petersen, *For Time or Eternity?* (Salt Lake City: Bookcraft, 1967), pp. 25–26. Ellipsis mine

Fifteenth President Gordon B. Hinckley taught, "Your chances for a happy and lasting marriage will be far greater if you will date those who are active and faithful in the Church."[3]

Kimball instructed LDS youth not to date until they were at least sixteen years old, "and even then there should be discernment."[4] While this age rule appears to have been followed religiously by many Mormon youth throughout the United States, the idea of dating only those in the church seems to have been relaxed. Rather, it seems that high moral behavior has become the main consideration. In a church youth magazine, an April 2010 article asked, "Should I date someone who is not LDS?" The answer? "Possibly, but don't date anyone (LDS or not) who, because of low standards, will drag you down."[5]

According to the leaders, this apparent open door for possibly dating those outside the church should only be practiced with those who have "high standards." Speaking to youth, sixteenth President Thomas S. Monson stated, "Begin to prepare for a temple marriage as well as for a mission. Proper dating is a part of that preparation. . . . Because dating is a preparation for marriage, 'date only those who have high standards.'"[6]

Many local LDS congregations host weekend dances and other social events to which their young people are encouraged to invite non-member friends. Non-Mormons often end up becoming attracted to the wholesome Latter-day Saints. Over the years I have counseled several Christian young people who have become involved in relationships with Latter-day Saints of the opposite sex. A non-Mormon who hopes to steadily date a Mormon may be pressured to participate in the missionary lessons and eventually join the LDS Church; otherwise, there may not be a chance to take the relationship to the next level. The Christian young person may recognize the falsehoods of Mormonism yet not know how to proceed without converting to Mormonism.

Christian researcher Sandra Tanner of Utah Lighthouse Ministry believes the problem is especially prevalent with those attending college. She said,

> I often get calls from Christian parents who are deeply concerned about their son or daughter because they have started to date a Mormon at college and have gotten involved in the LDS college social group. Often the person has joined the LDS Church without even telling the parents, informing them on their next school break. By that time, the person is often in a serious relationship that will lead to a temple wedding,

---

[2] Spencer W. Kimball, *The Miracle of Forgiveness*, pp. 241–42.
[3] *Ensign*, Nov. 1981, p. 41.
[4] Kimball, "The Marriage Decision," *Ensign*, February 1975, pp. 2–6.
[5] "Dating FAQs," *New Era*, April 2010, pp. 20–32.
[6] Monson, "Preparation Brings Blessings," *Ensign*, May 2010, p. 64. Ellipsis mine.

which the [non-LDS] parents will not be allowed to witness.[7]

I have seen far too many Christians reject their faith in order to pursue romantic relationships with Mormons. "Mixed faith" marriages are a recipe for disaster. In 2 Corinthians 6:14, Paul wrote, "Do not be unequally yoked with unbelievers. For what partnership has righteousness with lawlessness? Or what fellowship has light with darkness?" While Paul was not specifically talking about dating and marriage in this passage, he could have easily been referencing the lack of wisdom in such situations, especially since he had addressed the problems of mixed marriages earlier in 1 Corinthians 7:12–15.

I am of the opinion that a person is more likely to marry someone whom he or she *has* first dated. (Can you tell me how many married couples you know who didn't date first?) One thing that many young people don't think about is what will happen to their future children. Often the result is that the couple has to compromise, with the children dividing their attendance between two churches having major differences in doctrine. For adolescents, this can be confusing, to say the least. Therefore, it makes perfect sense for the faithful Christian believer to set the standards high from the very beginning.

Dating someone for the primary purpose of converting the other person (also called "missionary dating") is neither biblical nor ethical and should be avoided. While we are instructed to be "wise as serpents, and harmless as doves" (Matt. 10:16), dating a person in an attempt to change his or her religion is a wrong application of this passage. The ends do not justify the means.

Christians who emotionally manipulate Mormons for the purpose of conversion seriously jeopardize their integrity. Why should a Mormon want to follow the Bible when the Christian obviously is not following its teaching? To date (and then marry) someone from another faith (or no faith at all) is not God-honoring and invites tension in the relationship. The better policy is to refrain from dating those who could compromise your spiritual convictions.

---

[7] Sandra Tanner, e-mail message, July 21, 2010.

5 Points Overview of Chapter 8

1. Although some of the older LDS leaders didn't approve of their members dating those outside their faith, the current leadership appears to be OK with this as long as the other person is moral.
2. Even though two people may think they are "in love," they can never be on the same spiritual page if they are "unyoked."
3. If dating is the first step in a potential marriage, then consider both the character and spiritual nature of those you date.
4. The person you date and eventually marry will either help or hinder you in your personal walk with God. Always look for someone who will help you become a better Christian.
5. The person you date and eventually marry may become the parent of your child. Avoid conflict by keeping high standards.

Questions to Ask Your Mormon Friend

The Bible warns about the potential danger when becoming romantically involved with those outside the Christian faith. Because a worldview determines a person's thoughts and behavior, a faithful believer should not treat this issue lightly. If you have a friend who is involved in a relationship with a Mormon, it's important that you lovingly explain the biblical admonition to be "equally yoked," even in dating. Let the person know how much you care and, hopefully, biblical wisdom will take precedence over human emotions.

For those Latter-day Saints (or others outside the Christian faith) who might ask for you to go on a date, be nice but firm. Explain that while you value their friendship, you have purposely chosen to be picky about this issue. For you, dating someone of the same faith is important. Perhaps share some of the quotes given by LDS leaders as given in this chapter. Then ask,

> "While I appreciate your friendship, don't you think it could be dangerous taking our relationship to a dating level?"

Explain that you don't plan to convert to Mormonism and you certainly wouldn't want to pressure your friend to become a Christian just to keep a possible relationship alive. Indeed, the best policy is to save your dates for godly people within your own Christian faith.[8]

---

[8] For an article on this topic along with a three-part YouTube video series featuring my daughter Carissa, visit www.mrm.org/unequally-yoked.

Chapter 9: Examining the Ways of Sharing Your Faith with Mormons

For Christians who care about their faith, sharing Christianity with other people ought to be important. Whether those you know are atheists, Buddhists, or Hare Krishna devotees, the goal is to be effective in your witness.

Tactics and procedure do matter. For example, raising your voice to make a point can make you sound angry. Keeping your voice at an even level can be very winsome. In addition, there are topics that will be an immediate turn-off to most Latter-day Saints, such as attempting to speak to a Mormon about issues involving the temple (i.e. "What kind of underwear does a temple Mormon wear?" "What happens when you perform baptisms for the dead?" etc.). This could even be taken as offensive. Even if you have a solid relationship with the other person, I recommend staying away from these types of discussions.

We are often asked in this ministry, "What's the one question (or topic) that will convince a Latter-day Saint that Mormonism is wrong?" This is a request for a "magic bullet." Actually, it you ever discover a tactic that works most or all of the time that convinces Latter-day Saints of the truth, please let me know! With that in mind, here is a Top 5 list of ways that I find are most successful in sharing the Christian faith.

Step Number 1: Practice lifestyle evangelism

While the previous chapter explained why dating a Mormon is not a good idea, this doesn't mean you should avoid having friendships with Latter-day Saints. You may also have LDS family members and thus can't help but have a relationship with them, especially during holidays and family reunions.

One thing I have learned over the years is that some people outside your faith will closely watch you, especially if you publicly claim to be a Christian. How do you handle yourself when unfortunate circumstances arise? For example, do you lie to get yourself out of a tough situation? When offered a chance to cheat on a test, do you compromise your faith? People want to know if your faith is for real or if you are just another "hypocrite" who pretends to be a Christian.

When making friends or associating with others, you certainly want to avoid those who might cause you to compromise your faith. As Proverbs 15:33 says, "bad company ruins good morals." I wouldn't suggest that associating with Mormon people will corrupt your character! Instead, it might just challenge you to be a better owner of your faith, which was discussed in the third chapter. Being committed to living with a Christian world view is an important first step.

Step Number 2: Look for Opportunities...and ask lots of questions

If we end with Step Number 1, we fall short. The second step is searching for opportunities. This could happen in several ways, including the conversations we have with others. As humans, we typically like to talk about things that are important to us, including our faith. Suppose your friend says, "I went to church last night and . . ." Listen to what the other person says. (I have to admit that I too often interrupt others, not giving enough attention that is due.) Then ask questions:

- What did you learn at your meeting last night?
- Do you believe that (blank) is true? (If so, how do you know?)
- Where in the Bible do you believe it teaches such and such?

When it comes to spirituality, asking questions is a great way to learn about others and finding out their beliefs. People like to talk about themselves, so your questions provide them a chance to share. One thing you may discover is that they may not know very much about specific teachings of their church. At the same time, you might realize that you don't know very much about why you believe the way you do. Learn as much as you can about your own faith and then learn as much as you can about others.

An older friend of mine who converted to Christianity after belonging to the Jehovah's Witness religion for three decades used to say, "Error will always run from truth, but truth will never run from error." His saying is true. Don't be afraid to find out more about the Bible and what Christianity teaches, and don't be frightened to learn more about your friend's Mormonism. If you have questions on Mormonism, use our website (www.mrm.org). I recommend my friend Matt Slick's website (www.carm.org) for additional information.

Step Number 3: Create opportunities...and ask lots of questions

This is different from step number 2 because it requires an active role on your part. Instead of looking for opportunities, make your own.[1]

What are some ways you could do this? Here are just a few:

- Invite your friend to a fun night with your youth group or attend a special Christian event, such as a concert, together. Allow your friend to see what the people at your church are like. This could lead to further discussions on spiritual matters.

---

[1] Many of the ideas I list are best used with those of your same gender, as otherwise it might look like you are attempting to begin a romantic situation! It really is dangerous to attempt one-on-one evangelism with someone of the opposite sex, especially in the preteen/teen years.

- Invite your friend to join you at a fast food restaurant. Someone might think inviting a Mormon friend to Starbucks would be a better alternative, but you should remember that faithful Mormons don't drink hot drinks such as coffee and tea because of a health law called the "Word of Wisdom." A casual public place can provide the freedom to talk. Sometimes food and unlimited soda can make tense situations less stressful. (By the way, Mormons are allowed to drink caffeinated soft drinks, though some may still shy away from these as well.) As mentioned in the previous point, ask lots of questions. And share why you believe differently than what the Mormon Church leaders have taught.
- Invite your friend to read a book of the Bible with you (or host a group study with others). Explain how important reading the Bible is for you. Since you both believe the Bible is scripture, perhaps this would be a great way to deal with important issues. Choose a book like the Gospel of John. I am sure a youth pastor or another pastor at your church would like to be informed on how this goes.

Whichever possibility you choose, ask lots of questions and allow the Mormon(s) to explain why they believe something to be true.

Step Number 4: Share your personal testimony

All faithful Latter-day Saints are supposed to have a personal testimony that can be shared publicly with others. Your friend or the missionary at the door might start off by saying, "I testify to you that…" This is also called "bearing your testimony" and is something many Mormons practice. I suggest that you have your own testimony available to detail your beliefs and to explain why you believe your faith is based on the truth, not just subjective personal feelings.

Some Christians might get frightened when asked to share their stories, but this is nothing more than telling others what is very important in your life. Your testimony might not be very dramatic. For instance, you may not have a testimony of leaving drug dealing or a gang. It doesn't matter. What does matter is that it's *your* story of what God has done in your life. Most importantly, be genuine. While the Mormon is certainly entitled to his testimony, you have one too. Why not use it for the glory of God?

Step Number 5: Pray regularly for those you know

This could have very well been placed as step number 1. Don't think it's any lesser in importance because I've listed it last! If you are sharing your faith with other people, it's necessary that you do your best to explain biblical truth. Yet we cannot find success in our evangelism unless we bathe our words and testimony in prayer. The Bible says we are to "pray without ceasing." This doesn't mean we have to literally be mouthing words of prayer when we share our faith. At the same time, it does mean that successful evangelism requires a prayerful attitude.

Our job is in sales. We present the message in love with integrity to the best of our ability. Leave the production (conversion) to God. He is the One who is able to take our good work and bring people to a saving relationship with Him. What's really awesome is that He allows us to be part of this process! Pray regularly for your friend and be ready to be used by the King of the universe.

All in all, there is no formula in successful evangelism. Rather, it just requires a willing heart. How willing is your heart?

Warning: Many of the ideas I list below might be best used with those of your same gender, a might look like you are attempting to begin a romantic situation! It really is dangerous to atte evangelism with someone of the opposite sex, especially in the preteen/teen years.

Mormons are told that God told Joseph Smith about this health code, which is recorded in D&

Questions to Ask Your Mormon Friend

As explained in this chapter, asking your Mormon friends lots of questions (including, "Why do you believe that?" and "Where does it say that in the Bible?") can help you better understand what they personally believe. You may not always have exact answers, but you will learn how the other person thinks. The questions or points that stump you ought to be taken seriously. When in doubt, a possible response could be, *"That's a great question. Would it be OK if I went home and looked that up?"*

Then do it. Research the information in a book (maybe in your parents' or youth pastor's library) or on a Christian Internet site. Ask others for help. Don't be bashful. Whatever it takes, find out the answer. And then get back with the person who brought up the point or asked the question. It is amazing how God can use your faithfulness to create opportunities to share truth with other people.

Mormon Miracle Pageant in Manti, UT

For the last two weeks of June, hundreds of Christians gather in central Utah to share their faith outside the grounds of the Manti temple before the start of the Mormon Miracle Pageant. Here Carissa shares her faith with several teen girls in 2013.

Sharing your faith can take place in many different ways, including friendship evangelism (at school or with friends) or what is called "stranger evangelism," which involves getting into conversations with people in public places. At the Mormon Miracle Pageant where these pictures were taken, there are worship services / times of instruction at a local church throughout the two weeks. There is no better way to learn how to witness than doing it! Interested in coming next year? Go to www.mrm.org/mrm-manti for details. I'd love to meet you!

Photos courtesy of Terri Johnson and Mark Shreves

Conclusion: A Final Word to Christian Teens and Their Parents

I have been around long enough to understand that there are major challenges out there for our young people. Many of them are doing their best to determine the correct world view, whether or not it agrees with their Christian upbringing. If you are a Christian young person who is still trying to sort things out, I think that's perfectly fine. As I wrote in the first section of this book, I believe it's important for you to own your own faith. But there's going to be leg work involved! This could involve research and putting yourself on the line.

Jesus told a parable about the "pearl of great price." According to the story told by Jesus as found in Matthew 13:45-46:

> Again, the kingdom of heaven is like a merchant in search of fine pearls, who, on finding one pearl of great value, went and sold all that he had and bought it.

I have found that the times I have been most effective are when I do things outside my comfort zone. It might have involved standing outside a public event and handing out tracts while the majority of the passers-by rejected what I offered. Or having people drive by as they rudely yell out their car windows, "Get a life!"

Sometimes creativity works wonders. For instance, during the Christmas season of 2010 my friend Randy and I decided to dress up in Christmas costumes and see if we could give away "million dollar bill" tracts. Randy became "Santa" and I transformed into "Buddy the Elf" of the *Elf* movie fame.

After some trial and error, we discovered that visitors who come to Temple Square to see the Christmas lights loved what we were doing! I had memorized the important lines to the movie (For example, "Does somebody need a hug?" or "The three laws of the elves are: 1) Treat every day like Christmas; 2) There's room for everyone on the nice list; 3) The best way to spread Christmas cheer is singing loud for all to hear.") Sometimes it's hard to step out and be unique, but acting zany in a weird outfit worked! Families were willing to wait in line to have their pictures taken with us...for free!

The following year, we began producing personal "currency" with our photo on it along with a gospel message on the back. In a total of five years (through 2015), we have handed out more than 40,000 bills! In addition, we have visited the Ronald McDonald House, the Salt Lake Rescue Mission, Costco stores, and retirement

Since 2010, Santa Claus (Randy Sweet) along with the Grinch (Jamin McKeever), elves (including Elf Hannah in the front left), and Buddy (me) pose for photos outside Temple Square while distributing evangelistic "million dollar bills." The response is positive each night we go out! To see the website developed for this outreach (and found on the back of the tract), visit www.BuddyAndSanta.com. Photo by Terri Johnson.

homes on a number of occasions. The reaction we get is priceless. Meanwhile, the gospel is delivered through creative tracts while everyone has a great time. It's what they call a "win-win" situation.

Isn't the truth worth sacrificing everything in order to obtain the treasure? There can be nothing better than owning a faith that is true. And when you own it, you will want others to know too! The man who discovered the treasure in Jesus's parable was willing to do whatever it took to purchase the property and own the valuable treasure. Imagine what that person did after realizing he now owned the pearl. Wouldn't he want to tell everyone? I know I would.

Now it's your turn. After all, shouldn't our understanding of the sacrifice made by Jesus motivate us to want to share with others about our treasure?! If you are a follower of Christ, why not let others know about the most amazing gift anyone could ever receive? Life with Jesus is never boring. After all, He came to give us life (John 10:10). Cling to the promises made in the Bible and follow Him with every ounce of energy you have. And may the God of this universe bless you in your endeavors to glorify Him.

Appendix 1
Recognizing Poor Logic

In discussions with those who have opposing views, it is important to utilize sound reasoning skills. Sometimes, though, people resort to unfair tactics, which we call logical fallacies. Listed below are some common errors that you should learn to recognize and point out every time they are used.

Ad hominem: Criticizing a person who is making the argument rather than critiquing the argument itself. Ex: "Because John is a former Mormon, an apostate from the LDS Church, his anti-Mormon argument against the Book of Mormon cannot be considered valid."

> **Analysis:** Labeling someone negatively (such as "apostate" or "anti-Mormon") is meant to introduce a bias and should be avoided.

Appeal to pity: Attempting to sway the audience by using emotional tactics to gain sympathy. Ex: "Since Mormons have been persecuted throughout the years, this faith must be true or otherwise these people wouldn't have been attacked."

> **Analysis:** It is true that some Mormons have been persecuted over the past two centuries. This does not validate Mormonism's truth claims. If so, would the Mormon consider biblical Christianity to be true merely because Christians around the world are persecuted on a daily basis for *their* faith?

Appeal to the people: Insisting that your position is true because many other people agree with it. Ex: "The Church of Jesus Christ of Latter-day Saints has millions of members. Do you really think that many people can be wrong?"

> **Analysis:** Just because a lot of people share the same view does not guarantee that they are correct. If this is true, then perhaps Islam's billion-plus followers are correct in their assessment of spiritual truth.

Bandwagon: Believing a view is correct because of its popularity. Ex: "Since Mormonism is one of the fastest growing reli-

---

This appendix is taken from the appendix found in *Mormonism 101*.

gions, there must be some truth to it."

> **Analysis:** Even if it were true that Mormonism is "one of the fastest growing religions"—something that isn't even true—it needs to be understood that spiritual truth is *not* determined by popularity.

"Either or" fallacy/false dilemma: Claiming that "either" proposition A or B is true when a third option is possible. Ex: "If the Mormon Church isn't true, nothing else can be."

> **Analysis:** This statement that is sometimes used by faithful Latter-day Saints ignores the possibility of other options. If Mormonism isn't true, something else must be true, even if it's atheism, Buddhism, or Islam.

Faulty appeal to authority: Basing an argument on the opinion of a person or group. Ex: "I know for a fact that the Bible cannot be trusted. My bishop is a doctor and he said so."

> **Analysis:** This person's bishop may be knowledgeable in his particular field of expertise, but it does not necessarily mean he is an expert when it comes to the accuracy of the Bible. Looking at the evidence is more important.

Genetic fallacy: Rejecting an idea based on where it came from rather than on its merit. Ex: "I found this video critical of Mormonism on a website that is not sponsored by the Mormon Church, so it must be wrong."

> **Analysis:** Rather than criticizing the source of the information, the argument itself should be criticized.

Personal incredulity: Assuming that because something is difficult to understand, it must be untrue. Ex: "The doctrine of the Trinity is complicated and can't be comprehended. This proves it can't be true."

> **Analysis:** Trying to harmonize all the verses in the Bible that speak about God certainly involves in-depth study. But just because an explanation of something is not always simple does not make the premise false. There are many mysteries in Mormonism that also can't be understood, including matter that is eternal in nature or an eternal God who once was a human in another realm.

Red herring: Diverting the topic at hand by introducing an unrelated topic. Ex: After having a Christian share about salvation by grace through faith outside the grounds of Temple Square, an LDS person responds, "Do you share your faith at Muslim mosques or Buddhist temples? If not, why don't you go to those places instead of targeting Latter-day Saints?"

> **Analysis:** Getting off topic is a diversionary tactic meant to sideline the conversation. A possible reply is, "I'd be more than happy to talk about that issue, but could we first finish our conversation on salvation by grace through faith?"

Special pleading: Suggesting certain standards apply to others but not to oneself. Ex: "Yes, Doctrine and Covenants 1:31 does say that the Lord will not look upon sin with the least degree of allowance, but Heavenly Father loves me anyway and will allow me to be exalted."

> **Analysis**: Even though LDS scripture insists that no sin will be acceptable to God, those using this argument feel that they are somehow exempt from any penalty for their sin.

Straw man: Making a particular position look weak by misrepresenting the argument. Ex: According to *History of the Church* 6:476, Joseph Smith said the following: "Many men say there is one God; the Father, the Son and the Holy Ghost are only one God! I say that is a strange God anyhow—three in one, and one in three! It is a curious organization. . . . All are to be crammed into one God, according to sectarianism. It would make the biggest God in all the world. He would be a wonderfully big God—he would be a giant or a monster."

> **Analysis:** Smith gives an inaccurate analysis of what the Trinity teaches. Because it is not accurate, this version of the Trinity can be easily dismissed by the critic.

Conversations with your Mormon Friends

One of the most exciting things about learning new information regarding someone else's religion is being able to communicate better than before. At the same time, there can be dangers as well. For example, there is the possibility that your knowledge could be used to attack others. With that in mind, consider the following guidelines (as we have discussed) when having conversations with your LDS friends, family members, and classmates:

- *Don't assume that your Mormon friend believes the official Mormonism as taught by the leadership.* It is a mistake to tell someone, "You believe (such and such), so let me show you how you're wrong." To avoid this common error, always ask the Mormons what they believe about the issue at hand. "What do you believe about (XYZ)?" you might ask. Allow them to tell you what they really think. If you believe their view disagrees with the teachings of the LDS leaders, feel free to point out any inconsistencies, reminding them that the leaders have said that *they*, not the members, are qualified to define doctrine.

- *Be sure to define your terms.* Remember that the words used in Mormonism are very similar to those used in Evangelical Christianity. When your friend uses a term and you want to determine what is meant, ask, "What do you mean by (God/scripture/salvation/grace/baptism, etc.)?" You can use the definitions used at the beginning of the chapters in this book as a resource. Explain how your understanding of a term differs.

- *Be willing to listen.* Have you ever heard that a person has only one mouth but two ears? In other words, we should listen before we speak. A possible danger in understanding more about the background of Mormonism is that the Christian may want to use his or her knowledge to cut off the Latter-day Saints in mid-sentence without giving them the chance to be completely heard. Use eye contact and positive body language to show how they are being heard. Active listening skills go a long way in turning a possible 5-minute chat into an hour-long dialogue.

- *Don't think you have to be the world's expert.* Sometimes Christians think they have to be the experts on anything brought up in a conversation. Of course, everyone is limited in their knowledge. Don't be afraid to say, "I'm not sure what the answer to that question is. Let me find out and I will get back to you." Look up the information or talk to someone more knowledgeable. By being honest and not making up answers, you show integrity and will earn the right to be heard.

- *Be patient, kind, and real.* Your example is being watched closely by your friends and those around you. If you come across as arrogant, cocky, proud, and argumentative, your message may not be considered as carefully. Your attitude makes all the difference in the world.

Appendix 2
What must a person do in order to have a relationship with God?

With the exception of Christianity, all religions teach that there are certain requirements that must be met to reach a heavenly state. In effect, followers of other religions typically ask, "What must I do for my salvation?"

However, the Christian asks a much different question: "What did God first do for me?" The idea that salvation is a gift coming by grace through faith and not by works (Eph. 2:8-9) is a radical concept that is difficult for many to accept. We can summarize this teaching in just ten words:

God loves. A favorite verse for many Christians is John 3:16, which begins, "For God loved the world…" God's love for people is the motivating factor in how He deals with humanity.

Humans sinned. The Bible says that Adam and Eve introduced sin into the world. The consequence is that "death spread to all men, because all sinned" as there was "condemnation for everyone" (Rom. 5:13-18).

Jesus died. Jesus Christ came to this world with one purpose: to die on the cross and be raised back to life again. Romans 5:8 says, "But God proves His own love for us in that while we were still sinners Christ died for us!"

We believe. Romans 10:8b-10 says that "if you confess with your mouth, 'Jesus is Lord,' and believe in your heart that God raised Him from the dead, you will be saved. With the heart one believes, resulting in righteousness, and with the mouth one confesses, resulting in salvation."

God forgives. When we come into a relationship with God, our sins are washed away. Isaiah 1:18 teaches that "though your sins are like scarlet, they will be white as snow." This cleansing comes through the blood of Jesus, which brings "forgiveness of our trespasses" (Eph. 1:7).

I wrote this feature article for *The Apologetics Study Bible for Students* (Nashville, Holman: 2009), an excellent resource for those who want to learn more about their faith. Verses are quoted from the Holman Christian Standard Version of the Bible.

We cannot be justified before God by our works, as salvation is not like earning a paycheck. As Romans 4:6 puts it, "God credits righteousness apart from works." The story I gave in chapter 6 explains the role of works in salvation. Remember the grandfather who told his grandson that he was depositing "10" into the bank under his grandson's name? The young man didn't think anything of it until he decided to withdraw this money. When the teller gave him the requested $10 along with a receipt reporting that he had $9,999,990 in his account, he became confused and thought it was a joke.

While he thought he had just a few measly dollars, the grandfather had actually sacrificed everything to give him $10,000,000, an outrageous amount of money most people will never earn in their lifetimes. This present was not given as a *payment* but as a *gift*. Thus, when forgiveness is provided by God, it is a "done deal." Could there be any more of an awesome deal for the Christian believer?!

To have a relationship with Jesus, a person needs to understand the Gospel as described in the Bible. Here are six great references:

Acts 4:12: "*And there is salvation in no one else, for there is no other name under heaven given among men by which we must be saved.*"

Acts 16:30-31: "*Then he brought them out and said, 'Sirs, what must I do to be saved?' And they said, 'Believe in the Lord Jesus, and you will be saved, you and your household.'*"

Romans 3:28: For we hold that one is justified by faith apart from works of the law.

Romans 10:9-10: "*...because, if you confess with your mouth that Jesus is Lord and believe in your heart that God raised him from the dead, you will be saved. For with the heart one believes and is justified, and with the mouth one confesses and is saved.*

Galatians 2:16: "*...by works of the law no one will be justified.*"

Ephesians 2:8-9: "*For by grace you have been saved through faith. And this is not your own doing; it is the gift of God, not a result of works, so that no one may boast.*"

Appendix 3

10 Things an Investigator Ought to Consider Before Becoming a Mormon

Perhaps someone you know is thinking about joining the Mormon Church. If so, here are 10 reasons that ought to be considered before joining this religion. Share this with someone considering LDS baptism.

1. While Mormons may sincerely claim that "they're Christian too," it ought to be pointed out how the Mormon religion denies or distorts every fundamental teaching of the historical Christian church. Check out the essential doctrines denied in chapters 4-6.

2. Joseph Smith did not have integrity, as proven by his polygamous ways. A third of his 34 wives were married to living husbands and another third were teens. This type of immorality is not acceptable. See chapter 2.

3. There is no evidence that the Book of Mormon was produced on gold plates or that those who are portrayed in the Book of Mormon are real people. If this book is fictional, Mormonism is false. See chapter 5.

4. While Mormonism says that the atonement by Jesus on the cross is provided to all people, there are many requirements necessary for a person to have any hope of entering God's presence in the celestial kingdom. The problem is that there are so many requirements that are impossible to keep. See chapter 6.

5. Most converts get baptized a few weeks after beginning their lessons with the Mormon missionaries. It is probable that many do so for emotional reasons (perhaps to please family, friends, or even a potential spouse) without having a complete picture as to what the religion teaches. As with everything else (committing to a college, choosing a spouse, etc.), it is important to not have our emotions interfere with the decision-making process.

6. A person who gets baptized by the missionaries and is confirmed becomes an official member of the LDS Church. Getting

one's name off the official roll requires effort. It's like signing the paper's to a car loan—once you do this, it's difficult to turn back. How can you be sure you are making the correct decision?

7. The Mormon Church requires a person to tithe, or give 10 percent of one's total gross income, for a chance to attend an LDS temple. Ask yourself why this church has attached a financial requirement to salvation (the celestial kingdom) by requiring Mormons to tithe to get a temple recommend. Even Mormon 8:32 in the Book of Mormon says, "Yea, it shall come in a day when there shall be churches built up that shall say: Come unto me, and for your money you shall be forgiven of your sins." In addition, ask why the LDS Church does not release its financial statements, including how much the organization owns in stocks, bonds, land, and buildings as well as how much is received in members' tithes.

8. Ceremonies that take place in the temple are unbiblical, including baptisms for the dead and eternal marriages. Why would you join a church that requires its members to attend a temple and perform ordinances that are *not* biblically sound?

9. For many years, the Mormon Church did not allow those with black skin to become members in full standing. This is because priesthood authority was withheld from black men, which in effect prohibited them from having a chance to enter the celestial kingdom. It wasn't until 1978 that this priesthood ban was removed. Do some research and discover why the Mormon Church leaders were unfair to those with black skin, even insinuating that they had sinned in the preexistence and thus were given the "mark of Cain." For more information, see www.mrm.org/the-priesthood.

10. If you plan to purchase a new car, you would be foolish to listen *only* to the car dealer. You need to check with other sources, including a third party researcher such as *Consumer Reports*, to see if the product is all the dealer claims it to be. Do your "due diligence" by discovering potential problems and then make a sound decision. Faith of no substance is worse than no faith at all.

Appendix 4
7 Questions Your Mormon Friend May Ask (with responses)

1. Isn't it unchristian to question someone else's claim to Christianity? Aren't you judging when Jesus said not to do this according to Matthew 7:1?
- Didn't Joseph Smith question the "Christianity" of Bible believers when he claimed how God told him that the churches were "all wrong," that their creeds "were an abomination," and that their professors "were all corrupt" (Joseph Smith History 1:19)?
- Isn't your question a judgement on me? (Aren't you questioning me just as you say I'm questioning you?) We must also understand that, according to John 7:24, Jesus commanded Christians to "judge righteous judgment."

2. What about all of the fruit of the LDS Church, especially since it is the fastest growing church?
- Should numbers really determine truth? If so, perhaps there is a lot of truth to Islam since there are over one billion professing Muslims in the world.
- Are you suggesting that the Christian churches have no fruit? Consider the many philanthropic organizations, colleges, world relief, community support, etc. that have been founded and run by Christians. To say the Christian churches are not "fruitful" would be very naïve.

3. Don't you want to be with your family in the hereafter?
- If my family members are believers, we will be together in the afterlife. Heaven is a place made for all believers to have eternal fellowship with God.
- What guarantee do you have that you will exist with your family if your family members are not as righteous as you?

4. Don't you believe the true church needs prophets today?
- Why do you think a finite human should be our prophet when

For more questions that are often asked by Mormons with possible answers, check out the book Bill McKeever and I coauthored titled *Answering Mormons' Questions*.

there is a living prophet today? His name is Jesus. (Deut. 18:15 along with John 5:46, 6:14, 7:40; Acts 3:22-23, 7:37; Hebrews 1:1-2.)

5. What about the many errors of the Bible?
- Which "errors"? Are you sure that what you perceive to be an error is not just a lack of knowledge on your part? For additional information, visit www.carm.org/bible-difficulties.
- Are you bothered by how many changes have been made to the Book of Mormon since it was first published in 1830? See www.utlm.org/onlinebooks/pdf/introto3913changes.pdf.
- Why does your church expend so much time, effort, and money promoting and distributing the King James Version of the Bible to potential converts if it cannot be trusted?

6. Why is your pastor paid? (Doesn't that mean he's in the ministry for the money?)
- Why isn't your bishop paid? Even though Mormon "bishops" (like pastors) are not paid, D&C 42:71-73 say they should be. And according to D&C 75:24, missionaries are also supposed to be paid. Other LDS leaders are paid, including the general authorities and mission presidents (see www.mrm.org/mission-president-handbook).
- Would the fact that a number of people in the LDS Church—including many seminary teachers—receive "living expenses" and even salaries necessitate that they do this for the money?

7. If you say a person receives salvation based on faith alone, then what do you do with James ("faith without works is dead)? Don't you believe good works are important?
- I agree, faith without works is dead. A living faith produces works. However, a person's works can never be enough to have the power to forgive sins.
- Romans 3:28 says, "For we hold that one is justified by faith *apart from* works of the law."
- In the context of Eph. 2:8-9, verse 10 says the Christian is considered "God's workmanship," created to do good works.

Appendix 5
Why do so many former Mormons turn to atheism?

According to statistics, it is estimated that more than half of all former Mormons turn to agnosticism (the belief that the person is not sure whether or not a god exists) or atheism (the belief that there is no God). There may be several reasons why former Mormons reject Christianity and become attracted to agnosticism and atheism, including:

- Imagine if you found out that Christianity was not true. Wouldn't you be fearful of getting burned a second time? To some, non-religious possibilities may sound safer and more reasonable.
- A common catchphrase in Mormon circles goes like this: "If the (LDS) Church is not true, then nothing else is." This false idea is so engrained in the minds of many who decide to leave the Mormon Church that many naturally head toward agnosticism / atheism.
- Some become bitter when they discover how church leaders lied, so it is assumed that other churches must also deceive their members.

While my space is limited here, I can say that the evidence points to a Creator of the universe who is transcendent (above our thoughts). There are many excellent reasons to show how God does exist. Allow me to give you some book and Internet sources that can be understood by thinking teenagers and can be recommended if you know someone who is considering agnosticism or atheism.

- *The Case for Christ/The Case for Faith* (Harper Collins) by Lee Strobel. Written by a former atheist who interviewed scholars in his research.
- *I Don't Have Enough Faith to be an Atheist* (Crossway) by Norman Geisler and Frank Turek. This is a systematic treatment of God's existence by two Christian apologists.
- *The 10 Most Common Objections to Christianity* (Regel) by Alex McFarland. Provides answers to common questions asked by atheists.
- *Cold-Case Christianity* (David C. Cook) by J. Warner Wallace. A Christian police detective (a personal friend) uses his job experience to consider the truthfulness of Christianity's claims.

Also consider the following websites: www.carm.org, www.str.org, www.reasonablefaith.org, and www.godevidence.com, among many others.

Your prayers are appreciated!

To sign up for the Johnsons' free monthly newsletter titled "Johnsons' Great Adventures," please request it at eric@mrm.org. We can add you to the email or hard copy list...just say which you prefer.

May the Lord richly bless you as you serve the King of Kings!

Index: Mormonism 101 for Teens

Aaronic Priesthood: 9, 13, 16, 21, 76
Agency: 15
Anti-Mormon: 4, 94
Apostasy, Great: 10, 12, 16, 18
Articles of Faith: 53
Atonement: 56, 58-59

Baptism: 9, 18, 56, 58
Baptism for the Dead: 52, 71, 79
Bible: 48-50
Bible (errors): 103
Bishop: 71, 73
Bishop's Storehouse: 32
Blacks (Curse): 15, 52
Book of Abraham: 53-54
Book of Mormon: 19, 21, 27, 38, 50-51, 103
Born in the Covenant: 71, 79
Burning in the Bosom: 30
Branch: 71-73

Carthage Jail, 20, 23
Celestial Kingdom: 9, 16, 57-58, 66, 78-79, 100-101
Celestial Marriage: 9, 16
Chapel: 57, 71, 73
Church History Museum: 38
Commandments: 13, 33, 42, 46, 56-62, 66, 72, 77
Confirmation: 9, 18
Council in Heaven: 9, 15
Covenants: 13, 56, 58, 61
Cowdery, Oliver: 19, 21
Creeds (Christian): 12, 20, 102
CTR (Choose the Right): 71, 77

Dating: 83-86
Deacon: 9, 13
Doctrine and Covenants: 52-53
Elohim: See God the Father
Endowment: 65, 72
Enduring to the End: 7, 14

Especially for Youth: 71
Eternal Progression: 7, 11
Evangelism: 81-84
Exaltation: See Immortality

Family: 7-8, 30
Fastest Growing Church: 89
Fast and Testimony Meeting: 65, 68
Feelings, Good: 29
First Presidency: 1
First Vision: 17-18, 93
For the Strength of Youth: 71

General Authority: 7
General Conference: 1
Gift of the Holy Ghost: 11, 51-52
God the Father: 10, 12, 15, 20, 39-41, 46
Golden Contact: 9, 18
Gospel: 12, 15-16.56-57

Heavenly Father: See God the Father
Heavenly Mother: 41
Holy Ghost: 43
Hypocrite: 32-33, 87

Immortality: 10, 16
Independence, MO: 19, 21-22
Institute: 71, 77
Investigator: 10, 18

Jesus: 15, 19-22, 39--42, 44-45, 50, 56-58, 61-62
Judging: 102

Karma: 33
Lamanites: 19, 21, 50-51
Liberty Jail: 22
Logical Fallacies: 94-96
Lucifer: 11, 15, 41-42

Meetinghouse: 71-74
Melchizedek Priesthood: 10, 13, 21

Missionaries: 1, 3-5
Mormon (Book of Mormon): 19, 21
Mormon Miracle Pageant: 91
Moroni: 19, 21
Mortality: 10-11, 15
Mutual: 71, 76-77

Nauvoo, IL: 19, 22-24
Nauvoo Expositor: 20, 23
Nephites: 19, 21, 50

Ordinance: 56-58, 61
Outer Darkness: 10-11, 15

Paradise: 10, 15
Patron: 71-72, 77
Pearl of Great Price: 53-54, 74
Plan of Salvation: 13-16
Plural Marriage: See Polygamy.
Polygamy: 9, 20, 23-26
Premortality: 9-11, 13, 15, 33, 41, 56
Preexistence: See Premortality
Postmortality: 10, 13, 15
Priesthood (authority): 12
Priesthood (meetings): 74
Primary: 72, 74
Prophet: 1, 9, 23, 27-28, 74, 103
Proxy: 72, 77-78

Reformed Egyptian: 21, 51
Relief Society Meeting: 72, 74
Repentance: 56, 59-61

Sabbath: 32
Sacrament: 10, 13, 56, 58, 71, 73-74, 77
Sacrament Meeting: 72-73
Salvation: 56-66
Satan: See Lucifer
Seminary: 1, 72, 77
Smith, Emma: 26-28
Smith, Joseph: 1, 12-13, 19-

Biblical Index

27, 100
Sons of Perdition: 10, 15
Spirit Prison: 10-11, 15-16, 79
Stake: 72-73
Stake President: 72-73
Standard Works: 48-54

Teachings of Presidents of the Church (series): 74
Telestial Kingdom: 11, 16
Terrestrial Kingdom: 11, 16
Temple: 11-12, 15-16, 72, 77-80
Temple Recommend: 72, 78
Temple Square: 70
Testimony: 30-31, 74, 89-90
Tithe: 78, 101
Token: 78
Trinity: 43-45

War in Heaven: 11, 15
Ward: 71-73
Washing and Anointing: 72, 78
Word of Wisdom (Health Code): 52, 89
Works: 57-61

Young Women's Meeting: 72-74
Deuteronomy 6:4: 44, 47
1 Chronicles 17:20: 44
Psalms
   90:2: 46-47
   102:27: 41
Proverbs 5:33: 87
Isaiah
   1:18: 98
   6:8: 2
   43:10: 44, 46-47
   44:6, 8: 44
Malachi 3:6: 41, 47

Matthew
   1:18-25: 42
   7:1: 102
   7:15: 28
   10:16: 85
   10:37: 42
   13:45-46: 92
Mark 12:29-34: 47
Luke 1:35: 42
John
   1:1-3: 42, 47
   3:16: 98
   4:24: 46-47
   5:19: 42
   5:22: 42
   5:23: 42
   5:24: 62
   6:47: 47, 62
   7:24: 102
   8:32: 30
   10:10: 93
   14:1: 42
   14:28: 45
   20:28: 45, 47
Acts
   1:8: 42
   4:12: 47, 99
   7:59: 42
   13:39: 62
   16:30-31: 47, 99
   17:11: 28
Romans
   3:28: 47, 99, 103
   4:6: 99
   5:1: 62
   5:6-10: 42
   5:8: 98
   6:15: 63
   7:12-15: 79
   7:15-20: 61
   10:8-10: 98
1 Corinthians
   2:10-12: 43
   6:18: 28
   11:4: 42, 47
   15:3-4: 42, 47
2 Corinthians 6:14: 85
Galatians
   1:8-9: 28, 47
   2:16: 99
   4:16: 5
   5:4: 65
   5:19: 28
Ephesians
   1:7: 99
   2:8-9: 13, 47, 62, 98-99, 103
   2:10: 64
Philippians
   2:5-11: 42, 47
   3:9: 62
   4:7: 65
Colossians
   1:15-17: 42, 47
   1:19: 42
   2:9: 42, 47
1 Thessalonians 5:21: 47
1 Timothy
   2:5: 44
   3:2: 28
Titus 3:5-6: 47, 62
Hebrews
   1:6: 44
   2:18: 44
   8:12-13: 80
   9:11-15: 80
James
   1:5: 30
   1:17: 41
   2:14-26: 62, 103
1 John
   4:1: 28, 31, 47
   5:13: 47, 65
1 Peter 3:15-16: 47
Jude 1:3: 47
Jude 1:6: 10
Rev. 22:18: 54